Love Letters to the Lover of My Soul

Jan Eudy

Scripture quotations used in this book are from:

The Holy Bible, New International Version®.

ISBN: 1470154714

ISBN-13: 9781470154714

Library of Congress Control Number: 2012903916

CreateSpace, North Charleston, SC

INTRODUCTION

Why *Love Letters to the Lover of My Soul?*

These letters started out as my private response to God one morning during my quiet time. For some reason, I had a burning desire to write something to Him, a desire I had never had before. I can remember saying, "You wrote beautiful love letters to me in your Word. I want to write love letters back to you." That's how it all began.

The love letters that you are about to read do not come from spending thirty minutes a day with the Lord; they are a culmination of a lifetime of experiences with him. These letters reflect the high and the low points of a life spent loving the Lord but not always walking with him. They reflect obedience and, sadly, disobedience, and the loving way God draws us back to an intimate love relationship with him.

Different days, different feelings, different circumstances—they're all here. The pouring out of raw emotions to the one whom I know loves me, as well as my soul.

Being what it is, a collection of love letters, this writing can only be dedicated to the one that truly inspired me from start to finish, my Savior, Jesus Christ.

I also want to acknowledge my appreciation and love to my daughter Tiffany and son-in-law Mike, my granddaughters Ashley and Kaylee, as well as my dear friend Velta. Without their love, encouragement and support, this writing would never have made it to publication. I thank God for my entire loving family and many wonderful friends. You are all such a blessing.

As I read over these letters myself, there is no doubt in my mind who really wrote them. He is the true "Lover of my Soul."

Am I Significant?

Dear Lord,

Almost on a daily basis, I feel insignificant. Why am I here? Who cares if I'm here? But, then, if there's no significance to my life, why do you care how many hairs are on my head (Luke 12:7)? If I were insignificant, why would you promise never to leave me or forsake me (Hebrews 13:5)? If I were insignificant, why would you want to spend eternity with me and have even prepared a way for that to happen (John 3:16)?

What am I saying about you when I act and feel as if I have no value? My life is full of value and significance—why else would you allow me to be here? You have a purpose and plan for me and I am significant to you.

My significance is in you and you alone. My heart overflows with love and thankfulness to you, my God and my Savior, for making my life worthwhile!

Shared from the Heart

If we try to find our worth in anything other than God, we will fail. If we live our lives as if we do not matter, we are definitely "missing the boat."

People can put you down all day long but as long as you know that you are important to God, you can overcome anything. We might not understand everything that happens or the reason behind it, but we can trust the one that holds us in his hands and has a wonderful plan for each of his children.

Scripture Reading: Psalm 63:3-5

"Because your love is better than life, my lips will glorify you. I will praise you as long as I live and in your name I will lift up my hand. My soul will be satisfied as with the richest of foods; with singing lips my mouth will praise you."

"I AM a strong, beautiful authentic woman, a Daughter of Zion and I AM WORTHY!"

Where's the Beauty?

Dear Lord,

Sometimes I look at the world and only see ugliness. I see us, your children, putting everything before you, our Creator. I see people that have absolutely no respect for human life and do not care about what you think at all. I see our entertainment world having total disregard for you and doing their very best to persuade the world to believe that everything is okay—there's no right or wrong. Such ugliness!

But then I look into the face of my grown child and I see her love for you—pure beauty. I look into the face of my granddaughters and I see a wonderful excitement about life and I'm reminded about your love for them—pure beauty. I look at the beauty you gave us in all of nature and I'm reminded that *"all good things come from you"* (James 1:17).

Last but not least, I look at the cross and I see the ultimate beauty—the sacrifice of your Son so that I might see you one day in all your splendor and beauty.

Thank you, Lord, for your "everyday" beauty. Help me to see it and praise you for it!

Shared from the Heart

Yes, our society seems to be "going down the tubes," morally speaking, but every day there is something beautiful that God wants to show us. It may come in the form of something as simple as a blue sky, a snowy mountain, or the laughter of a small child.

Look around and let God show you something beautiful in his creation. It's there; sometimes we just have to pay closer attention.

***Scripture Reading:* Nehemiah 9:6**

"You alone are the LORD. You made the heavens, even the highest heavens, and all their starry host, the earth and all that is on it, the seas and all that is in them. You give life to everything, and the multitudes of heaven worship you."

The Beauty I See

Can I Make It?

Dear Lord,

There are times the heavy load of life gets me down so far that all I want to do is crawl up in your lap, put my head on your shoulders, and weep. It just doesn't seem like it's worth it. I'm tired, I'm weary, and I'm pretty worn!

The security of sitting in your lap can be mine all day long. All I have to remember is that I am never alone and I never have to face anything that comes my way that you haven't provided the guidance and strength to endure.

Paul said in Philippians 4:13, *"I can do everything through Christ who gives me strength."* I CAN be an overcomer—not in my own strength but in yours. All I have to do is trust in you, in your power, and in your faithfulness. AND TRUST YOU I WILL because you, God, are faithful!

Shared from the Heart

More than likely, there will be a time in everyone's life that we feel like we "just can't go on." We might feel weighed down because of a tragedy that has touched our lives or just because life, for some reason, has become too tiresome and too wearisome.

Take heed; we do not have to be consumed. There is one who loves us more than life itself and is faithful. Simple trust is all he asks from us; the rest is his job.

Scripture Reading: Lamentations 3:22-23

"Because of the LORD's great love we are not consumed, for his compassions never fail. They are new every morning, great is your faithfulness."

Deep Joy

Dear Lord,

When I look at my life as a whole, what I see is a little unsettling and not totally pleasing. Career-wise, I really didn't climb too much of the ladder; talents are not in over-abundance; financially, I could have made a few better decisions; and relationships—a few failures there.

So, why is it I'm not totally depressed and miserable? Because of you, Lord. Because I gave you my life and you take that seriously. *"The joy of the LORD is my strength"* (Nehemiah 8:10).

When you look at me, you don't see a failure. You see one of your precious children that is clean and righteous before you. Not righteous because of anything I did or accomplished but because when you look upon me, you see Jesus.

Satan tells me I'm a failure but you tell me I'm your child and you are my Father (I John 3:1). Now, if that's not a reason for heartfelt joy, I don't know what is!

I love you, Father.

Shared from the Heart

If we measure ourselves by the world's standards, we could be labeled a "failure" and that's pretty depressing. If we measure ourselves by God's standards, once we have given our lives to Christ, we are labeled "his children" and that in itself should fill us with deep and everlasting joy.

Scripture Reading: Psalm 21:6

"Surely you have granted him eternal blessings and made him glad with the joy of your presence."

Blessed!

Dear Lord,

When the word "blessed" comes to my mind, my first thoughts are of material things (sorry, but it is true). But then as I allow the Holy Spirit to guide my thoughts, I see so much more in "blessed." This is what I see:

- I know you, the one true God (Jeremiah 10:10).
- I feel the blessing of what you accomplished on the cross (Romans 5:8).
- I am blessed as your Holy Spirit fills me (Matthew 5:6).
- The ultimate blessing: "*Blessed is he whose transgressions are forgiven, whose sins are covered. Blessed is the man whose sin the LORD does not count against him and whose spirit there is no deceit*" *(*Psalm 32:1-2*)*.

There's a song that goes something like this: "Count your blessings, name them one by one, count your many blessings and see what God has done." What a wonderful song and what a wonderful way to start my day and not a bad way to end it, either.

Count my blessings and "thank you" one by one. I am truly one blessed woman!

Shared from the Heart

Blessings do not always come in monetary form. Many times we fail to see all of the wonderful blessings the Lord gives us on a daily basis.

For some people, just being able to get out of bed in the morning is a major blessing. We should never go a day without counting our blessings and thanking him for each and every one.

Scripture Reading: Jeremiah 17:7-8

"Blessed is the man who trusts in the LORD, whose confidence is in him. He will be like a tree planted by the water that sends out its roots by the stream. It does not fear when heat comes; its leaves are always green. It has no worries in a year of drought and never fails to bear fruit."

Scared/Overwhelmed?

Dear Lord,

When I become anxious about the future and even the day-to-day living and I let all this build up inside me, you place your Word before me and show me what you went through. You show me in Philippians 2:8 how you humbled yourself and was obedient unto death. Nothing I could possibly go through compares with what you endured for me–for my eternal comfort and good.

Help me, Lord, to humble myself before you. Being humble before you at the same time that I'm scared to death or completely overwhelmed doesn't sound like it goes together but I believe it does. James 4:10 says: "*Humble yourselves before the Lord, he will lift you up.*" When I humble myself before you, I am telling you that I am relying totally on you and not on myself.

There's no way to say I totally understand but I can say "thank you" with the way I live my life—a life lived in humility, thankfulness, and gratitude.

Shared from the Heart

Sometimes life is just flat overwhelming. When this happens, we have two choices in dealing with this feeling. We can either let it take over and pull us further down or we can choose dependence—dependence on the only one who is able to calm our fears and our anxiety and lift us up. We have to rely on the one true God, who will never leave us or forsake us no matter the circumstances.

Scripture Reading: Psalm 94:19

"When anxiety was great within me, your consolation brought joy to my soul."

Sinning

Dear Lord,

Why do the same sins keep creeping up time after time? Don't you get tired of hearing the "same old confessions"? I hope not!

I John 1:9 says: "*If we confess our sins, he is faithful and just and will forgive our sins and purify us from all unrighteousness.*" When I confess, it is with a repentant heart and I do make an effort to overcome things that should not be in my life. So, what do I have to remember here? I must remind myself that:

- I am human and will mess up (but I won't use that as an excuse).
- You will forgive me no matter what and no matter how many times.
- There is always forgiveness but sometimes sin does bring discipline (Revelation 3:19).
- You will remember my sins no more (Hebrews 8:12).

Life as a believer is not always easy but it is rewarding. You reward me every morning with a new and clean slate. You give me undeserved forgiveness and love. I can't earn it; it's a free gift.

What I need to do every morning is ask you to empty me of all the "yucky" stuff I've accumulated over the last twenty-four hours and fill me with you—empty self and fill with the Holy Spirit.

Shared from the Heart

Don't you just hate it when you ask for forgiveness for a sin and then down the road you find yourself committing the same sin again? You know you were truly repentant the first time but here you are again, having to ask for forgiveness one more time.

We have to remember that God will always forgive us but he doesn't stop there. If we sincerely want to overcome sin, he will give us the strength, wisdom, and guidance we need if we will only listen, trust, and rely on him.

Scripture Reading: Ephesians 2:8-9

"For it is by grace you have been saved, through faith—and this not from yourselves, it is the gift of God—not by works, so that no one can boast."

Safe, Secure, and Loved

Dear Lord,

Circumstances change, people change, love fades but what keeps me going is the truth that you, dear God, do not change (Malachi 3:6). Time after time in your Word you tell me you will never leave me (Deuteronomy 31:6, Hebrews 13:5, Joshua 1:5) and you are the only one that can make that promise and never break it.

How safe I feel knowing that the Creator of all things cares enough about me to go with me wherever I go (Joshua 1:9). How secure I feel knowing that nothing can separate me from your love.

The answer is yes, there's no doubt about it—I am safe, secure, and definitely loved!

Shared from the Heart

We will receive many promises from people in our lifetimes. A lot of these promises will be broken one way or the other.

God is the only one who, when he promises, will not and cannot break that promise.

Read his Word and bask in his promises, knowing that he alone is faithful to the very end and beyond.

Scripture Reading: Romans 8:38-39

"For I am convinced that neither death nor life, neither angels nor demons, neither the present nor the future, nor any powers, neither height nor depth, not anything else in all creation will be able to separate us from the love of God that is in Christ Jesus our Lord."

Do You Love Me?

Dear Lord,

Are you asking me if I love you? My first response would be like Peter's—"*Yes, Lord, you know I love you*" (John 21:15). But let's look deeper in my heart, beyond the emotional answer. Do my actions reflect my answer? Am I doing what you told me to do in Mark 12:31-32? Am I loving you with all my heart, soul, mind, and strength? Am I loving my neighbor as myself?

The first part of the question is a little easier than the second part. I know I love you but that second part—love my neighbor as myself—that part doesn't come as easily. That takes actual work, actual effort. Putting the needs of others before your own is not the natural instinct. Me first and then others, that's the human way. But, like a lot of other things, I have it backwards—put others first and you will take care of me. You always have and you always will.

Loving others isn't always easy but if you tell me to do it then I can do it. You don't command me to do something and then make it impossible to accomplish, and that includes loving others as myself!

Shared from the Heart

For some people, loving others is easy and just part of who they are. There are some of us for whom loving others takes more effort but the ability to love is there; we just have to dig a little deeper inside and "tap into" it. God doesn't tell us to love others without giving us the capability to love, even the hard-to-love.

God loves us and wants that love returned, not only to him but to everyone.

Scripture Reading: 1 John 4:19-21

"We love because he first loved us. If anyone says, 'I love God,' yet hates his brother, he is a liar. For anyone who does not love his brother, whom he has seen, cannot love God, whom he has not seen. And he has given us this command: Whoever loves God must also love his brother."

Your Way

Dear Lord,

I'm minding my own business, getting along quite nicely, and, WHAM, here comes a pretty hefty-size problem to deal with. I let it get the best of me and then I fall on my knees and cry out for help like David did in Psalm 5:2.

Why is it so easy to panic and forget that nothing is coming my way that you don't already know about? I don't ever have to deal with anything alone.

We are taught that we should *"consider it pure joy..."* (James 1:2) when problems come our way. Is that easy to do? NO WAY, but it is your way. You can do so much for others when we are willing to let you use us through our difficulties.

Your ways are always higher than my ways. What I consider terrible experiences and ones I would like to forget, you consider as ways to help others. I need to share experiences so others can see how faithful and true and trustworthy you are.

God, please help me to relax in you, trust in you, and believe your Word. It all comes down to TRUST in you and in your ways.

Shared from the Heart

God can use anything to help other people. Maybe the difficult experiences in our lives need to be shared with someone who is going through the same thing and can't see how they will make it to the other side in one piece. By sharing, we are a witness of God's faithfulness and provision for all who seek him.

Scripture Reading: Isaiah 26:3-4

"You will keep in perfect peace him whose mind is steadfast, because he trusts in you. Trust in the LORD forever, for the LORD, the LORD, is the Rock eternal."

Where Are You?

Dear Lord,

I don't hear you. I don't feel you, Lord. So, where are you? You promised to never leave me (Hebrews 13:5); are you keeping your promise? I have some really big problems to solve and I'm not hearing you.

All this is welling up inside of me and then I hear your soft nudging, *"Be still and know that I am God"* (Psalm 46:10). Right now that is really hard to do Lord. Be still? What do I do about all these problems? I have a lot of questions and I'm not sure what the right answers are. "*Be still and know that I am God.*" Is that all you have to say? YES!

Shared from the Heart

Let's face it: most of us think that we have to be "doing" something when problems arise in order to "fix" them. This is not always true. Sometimes we have to take a step back, be still, and listen to God. If we don't, more than likely our solutions will not be the right ones.

So remember to be still—God alone has the right solutions and he won't keep them from you, but you have to be listening.

Scripture Reading: Psalm 62:1-2

"My soul finds rest in God alone; my salvation comes from him. He alone is my rock and my salvation; he is my fortress, I will never be shaken."

Attitude

Dear Lord,

Sometimes I start my day with a "defeated" attitude. I wake up in the morning and think, "What day is it? Oh, it's just Tuesday. I have to get up and go to work. YUCK!" I should be waking up and saying, "Praise the Lord, it's another chance to glorify God."

I will face each new day with an attitude. I will either begin my day with a victorious attitude trusting that anything that comes my way can be overcome by the power of the Holy Spirit that lives within me or I can begin my day with an attitude of defeat, not expecting anything special to happen in me or through me—just another day… big deal!

Thank you, Lord, for reminding me that I am not defeated. I am a victor; because you have overcome (John 16:35), I can. Help me to live in your power day by day, hour by hour, and minute by minute.

I am overcome with your love for me!

Shared from the Heart

Wouldn't it be great to intentionally start our day "in the power of the Holy Spirit"? We can. It's ours for the taking.

Think of the good we could accomplish in one day if we would only remember that, as believers, the Holy Spirit lives within us and will provide all the power, strength, and wisdom we need. All we have to do is rely on that power and then act upon it.

Scripture Reading: Isaiah 40:29-31

"He gives strength to the weary and increases the power of the weak. Even youths grow tired and weary, and young men stumble and fall; but those who hope in the Lord will renew their strength. They will soar on wings like eagles; they will run and not grow weary, they will walk and not be faint."

Forgiveness

Dear Lord,

Sometimes I feel like I'm giving my very best but I'm getting nowhere. What I call my "ministry" isn't growing. I don't see changes in people's lives that are in my sphere of influence. There's something missing and I'm not sure what it is. What's the deal?

I see what the deal is as you gently reveal to me the truth that there is an unresolved problem with a fellow believer that must be dealt with immediately. I may feel I've been wronged but he may be feeling the same way. That relationship needs mending. Maybe that relationship cannot be what it once was because of different opinions or different perspectives but it can be made right. I must go to my brother (fellow believer, if at all possible) and ask for forgiveness for anything he feels I have done and to forgive him (Mark 11:25).

Forgiveness is like a deep cleaning—it gives back the joy of our salvation and we can once again be a usable vessel. I cannot let pride rob me of that freedom and joy.

Forgiveness started with you, Lord; now I must follow and forgive and also ask for forgiveness in return.

Shared from the Heart

Someone once said, "The only person you are hurting when you hold back forgiveness is yourself." That is a true statement.

Until we put aside our pride and offer forgiveness, there will always be that uneasy feeling deep down inside. The moment we realize that forgiveness is the right thing to do and we actually do it, the freedom we will feel is amazing.

Sometimes, however, when we offer forgiveness, we in turn need to ask for forgiveness. It is a two-way street.

Scripture Reading: Matthew 5:23

"Therefore, if you are offering your gift at the altar and there remember that your brother has something against you, leave your gift there in front of the altar. First go and be reconciled to your brother; then come and offer your gift."

Best Friend!

Dear Lord,

"What a Friend We Have in Jesus", what a beautiful song. What a beautiful thought—Jesus, my best friend. There's no one who knows me the way you do. You know me better than I know myself. You know if I'm going to help our friendship grow, or if I'm going to cause our friendship to grow stale, or even if I'm going to walk away from our friendship for a while (past experiences).

"*A true friend loves at all times...*" (Proverbs 17:17). You have blessed me with many wonderful friends but you are the only one who can promise that he will never leave or forsake me (Hebrews 13:5) and keep that promise. It feels good to know that I am truly never alone and that I can talk to you anytime I want. I love just having a normal conversation with you because I can be totally myself, no façade, just the real me. You don't care if I mispronounce words and you don't care that I don't always make sense when I talk. I can be as serious or as funny as I want. I love it when I say something funny and I feel you laughing with me. That's what best friends do—they laugh together, they cry together, and they are always there when you need them.

You, Lord, are my best friend!

Shared from the Heart

Friends are a wonderful gift but a "best" friend is something really special.

It's hard to call someone your best friend if you can't confide in them your deepest feelings, fears, and hurts. It would also be hard to call someone your best friend if you never spent quality time with them.

Jesus can be our Savior and, as a bonus, we can have the perfect "best friend" ever!

Scripture Reading: John 15:15

"I no longer call you servants, because a servant does not know his master's business. Instead, I have called you friends, for everything that I learned from my Father I have made known to you."

16. You did not choose me, I chose you, and I want you to go and share the good news of the love I have given to you so that, no matter what you ask for, if you ask in my Father's name, it will be given to you! John 15:15-16 ♥NJV♥

Falling in Love!

Dear Lord,

There have been so many times in my life that I would have to say I was living a "hypocritical" lifestyle. I was faithful in a lot of things but I still allowed the desires of this world to rule my life. But, Lord, I can say to you from the sincerest part of me that I can see that this has changed. I can look back and see what happened. What happened to change my desires was that I actually fell madly and deeply in love with you.

I didn't just change because I wanted to do things right or to please you…well, maybe to please you, but mainly because you became my one "true" love. It took me a long time to get to this place and it was a long, bumpy road but, through your grace, you got me here.

How do you know you love someone? When you crave spending time with them; when you can't wait to talk to them; when what they have to say is important to you; and when you have no fear or anxiety about being yourself with this person.

Loving and pleasing you are all I want. Please never let that change. Let me always do as you commanded in Matthew 22:37, *"Love the Lord your God with all your heart and with all your soul and all your mind."*

I love loving you and being loved by you!

Shared from the Heart

In one of her Bible studies, Beth Moore with Living Proof Ministries once said that her prayer for her daughters was that they would fall deeply and madly in love with Jesus. I love that.

When we fall deeply in love with someone, we want nothing more than to put them first in our lives.

What would our life look like if Jesus were first in everything?

Scripture Reading: John 14:21

"Whoever has my commands and obeys them, he is the one who loves me. He who loves me will be loved by my Father and I too will love him and show myself to him."

Control

Dear Lord,

Why do I think I can run my life better than you? When I try to take control, the peace that is usually mine disappears.

Nobody loves me like you do and nobody knows better than you what directions I need to take. That realization will get me through whatever life brings my way if you are doing the leading. Of course, my life wouldn't have had as many "bumps" in it if I had allowed you to be my pilot and not my co-pilot all these years. I find it easier to give you control after I've totally messed up the situation. Then, I just want you to "fix it."

Life's "ups and downs" (physical or emotional) are so much easier to handle when I lay my heart open before you and trust in your loving care. Trust as in Lamentations 3:22: *"Because of the LORD's great love we are not consumed."*

If I've only learned one thing in life, that one thing would have to be: I'm not in control but, thanks be to God, you are! And, believe me, Lord, I don't want control any longer!

Shared from the Heart

There were times in my life when I felt "out of control." I made decision after decision on my own without asking for help. Needless to say, these decisions usually were not the right ones and sometimes made things worse.

With God's help and guidance through the years, I have learned that the wisest thing for me to do is to start my day, every day, giving authority over to him. Things just seem to turn out better with him controlling and me following. I learned that lesson the hard way!

Scripture Reading: Deuteronomy 33:12

"Let the beloved of the LORD rest secure in him, for he shields him all day long and the one the LORD loves rests between his shoulders."

Decisions—Pray or Jump?

Dear Lord,

When I face big decisions in my life, I don't have any problem talking to you about them and seeking your wisdom and guidance. I am able to do what the psalmist says in Psalm 37:5: *"Commit your way to the LORD; trust in him."*

Then there are those decisions that I just seem to "jump" into all by myself without talking to my best friend and the one person who truly cares about my life: YOU.

Does it break your heart, Lord, when I just "use" you for the big deals and act like I don't want to include you in all areas of my life? I guess I choose what I want to include you in and leave you out of those "small enough for me to handle all by myself" decisions. Sometimes I think I am so wise!

What is it going to take for me to learn that you should be and want to be the first one I discuss everything with, no matter what it is or the size? You want this because I am precious to you and you care like no one else can. Psalm 139:9-10 says: "*If I rise on the wings of the dawn, if I settle on the far side of the seas, even there your hand will guide me, your right hand will hold me fast.*" When you love, you love with all you have, which covers me entirely—big and small.

Father, help me to not just jump into decisions unless it is you that says, "Jump."

Shared from the Heart

I happen to believe that God wants to be involved in every part of my life. He's not just interested in the "big" stuff but "all" my stuff.

I know through experience that his ways have better results than when I ignore our relationship and make decisions without consulting him. Another one of my hard lessons learned!

Scripture Reading: Haggai 1:5

"Now this is what the LORD Almighty says: 'Give careful thought to your ways.'"

Do I Look Different?

Dear Lord,

When people look at me, do they see something different? Do they see you? If they don't see you, I'm not the person you desire me to be.

You are a hard act to follow. You are perfect in all ways. But perfection is not what you are looking for, is it? It's my efforts and my desire to strive toward perfection or pursue righteousness. I will always fall short but as I travel on through this life, and as I give you my all—every part of me—others and I will be able to see change…not only change in my actions and reactions but change in the very desires of my heart, where it all starts. Psalm 37:4 says, *"Delight yourself in the LORD and he will give you the desires of your heart."*

I want the unbelieving world to look at me and say, "I want what she's got." What I want them to want are my peace and my love for others that can only come from you.

Help me, Lord, to look and act different from the inside out!

Shared from the Heart

I want to look different. I want my face to reflect what God has put on the inside: a peace that surpasses all understanding.

I believe there's a difference in putting on a "happy face," pretending everything is just great, and allowing God's peace to shine through us, no matter the circumstance.

Scripture Reading: Matthew 5:8

"Blessed are the pure in heart, for they will see God."

Your Book

Dear Lord,

Your holy Word is so powerful, so full of wisdom and truth. There were times when I thought I saw inconsistencies but if I took the time to either search deeper into it myself or talk to someone who has studied your Word in depth, your Word always stands without contradiction. You said, *"All scripture is God breathed"* (2 Timothy 3:16) and I believe it.

There are times when it's not always "easy" reading but if I keep my mind and heart open, you will always show yourself.

It's overwhelming as I realize that this glorious book was written to help me thousands of years later. Romans 15:4 says: *"For everything that was written in the past was written to teach us, so that through endurance and the encouragement of the Scriptures we might have hope."*

My life would be a total mess if I didn't believe without a doubt that your Word is you, my Creator, talking and loving me, your child.

It's not just a history book or an instruction book; it's a snapshot of who you really are!

Shared from the Heart

Sometimes we forget what a valuable possession we have in our Bible. Believe it or not, there is an answer to all of life's questions in this book. Yes, sometimes it takes time to find it but when you do, it is time well spent.

A lot of people say that the Bible is outdated and not relevant to society today. Get real. God is God. He certainly wasn't going to write something that would have a time limit on it. He knew what we needed way back then and he knows what we need today.

Scripture Reading: Psalm 1:1-2

"Blessed is the man who does not walk in the counsel of the wicked or stand in the way of sinners or sit in the seat of mockers. But his delight is in the law of the LORD and on his law he meditates day and night."

Growing Older

Dear Lord,

As I ponder my life, I see a lot of change: good change and not-so-good change. As I reach another decade of life, I see one thing very clearly: I've changed, people around me have changed—change is everywhere. The only thing that does not change is you. Malachi 3:6 states, *"I am the LORD, I do not change."*

I heard someone say one time, "She didn't grow old very gracefully." I hope that is never said about me. I don't want them to think I'm "mellowing out" just because I'm growing older. I want to seem mellower because of the peace and assurance I have through my relationship with you—the kind of peace that will carry me through to the other side. Aging isn't always fun and it isn't always easy but it certainly can be a blessing. I can't believe I just said that!

I will praise you during all changes in my life. I will be content as wrinkles appear, as my body sags, and when memories start to fade, knowing that no matter what I face in the aging process, you are ALWAYS there!

Shared from the Heart

I really don't believe that worrying about getting older makes a lot of sense. If you are breathing, you are going to get older. If you are going to age with grace, there's one thing you have to accept: change. Everything changes. Your body changes, your mind changes, finances can change, and sometimes our attitudes change.

With all these changes, there is one thing we can depend on not to change and that is our God. He is faithful to keep his promise that he will never leave us no matter what our age is. That will never change.

Scripture Reading: Philippians 1:6

"Being confident of this, that he who began a good work in you will carry it on to completion until the day of Christ Jesus."

Unforgiveness/Forgiveness

Dear Lord,

Why in the world must I drag up such ancient memories just because I'm studying about forgiveness? This happened over thirty-five years ago. I'm way past that. I've had all kinds of things happen to me between then and now. Why should I even think about this now? This person will never even know I've released her with my forgiveness. What's the point?

The point is telling you I forgive her specifically doesn't release her as much as it releases me. I've gone back so many times in my life and searched for things that maybe I haven't asked for forgiveness for so that there would be nothing between you and me. But with all this time passed, I never really gave a whole lot of thought about my having to forgive someone else.

Yes, someone who hurt me badly and changed my life big-time so many years ago can still affect who I am today. Forgiveness is a two-way street: I forgive, you forgive me. That's very plain in your Word. Matthew 6:14 says, *"For if you forgive men when they sin against you, your heavenly Father will also forgive you."*

I expect you to forgive me, every time I ask you, without hesitation. Why? Because you are faithful and will do what you say. You also say in Mark 11:25, *"When you stand praying, if you hold anything against anyone, forgive him, so that your Father in heaven may forgive you your sins."* There is a condition there that I pass over without even realizing it. I cannot hold unforgiveness in my heart and be forgiven—that's just not the way you work and you keep your word, every time.

My prayer, Lord, is that I will never harbor unforgiveness in my heart. All that does is put "junk" between you and me. A pure heart is my heart's cry.

Shared from the Heart

I believe that holding a grudge against someone and not forgiving them can slowly eat up our insides (spiritually speaking). Sometimes it takes a long time to let something go but the result is worth it.

It's not always possible to forgive someone in person but we can offer that forgiveness through the Lord. He knows our hearts and he will take care of the rest.

Scripture Reading: Psalm 40:8

"I desire to do your will, O my God, your law is within my heart."

july 1, 2017

Who's Talking Anyway?

Dear Lord,

I love it when you prove yourself to me in such a wonderful way.

Witnessing, as you know, is difficult for me. I know that the way I live my life is a major witnessing tool for me but you have told me in your Word to always be prepared to give the answer for the hope within me (1 Peter 3:15). When I feel the Holy Spirit's "nudging" me to talk to someone about you, I begin to feel a little nervous or anxious inside. I try to rationalize the way to do it: ignore it (it wasn't really God), send an email or a letter—anything but person to person. But sometimes what you need us to do is give someone that "personal" touch for you.

Glory be to God, when I was obedient you did exactly what you did for Moses in Exodus 4:11-12. You spoke for me. I could not have said the things I did by myself—you took over. You knew what that person needed to hear, not me. If left on my own, I would have gone off on the "end times" prediction and tried to scare him to death. But, you, O Lord, are so wise and know where to touch the very place someone needs to be touched.

Thank you for always being my faithful and caring God and confirming, once again, that because of Christ you do dwell within me and you will never make me speak on my own. You are faithful and true.

Shared from the Heart

Personally witnessing to someone, especially to family, is not easy, at least not for me. I have learned through the years that if I'm obedient and witness when I know deep down inside that it's what I'm supposed to do, God is always faithful. He will tell me what to say—how much and how little to say. All he wants from me is my willingness.

Scripture Reading: John 15:10-11

"If you obey my commands, you will remain in my love, just as I have obeyed my Father's commands and remain in his love. I have told you this so that my joy may be in you and that your joy may be complete."

Security

Dear Lord,

I love feeling safe and secure and I don't like it when I feel the opposite. I can put all the locks and bolts I want to on my doors (if that were necessary); I can take all kinds of safety precautions but I really feel "safe and secure" when you and I are walking side by side. I love it when I read in your Word about you holding my hand (Isaiah 41:13) and about you being my hiding place (Psalm 32:7).

There's no better feeling in the world than knowing that nothing can separate us (Romans 8:38-39) and that no one can snatch me out of your strong hands (John 10:28-30).

I am most secure in the shadow of your wings. What a place to be!

I am depending on the perfect security system—the one and only Jesus Christ.

Hand

Isaiah 41:13

Shared from the Heart

When I was younger, I was terribly afraid of the dark. If you've ever had that fear, you know what a horrible feeling it is. It took years but as the Lord and I worked through it, he reminded me of several promises that would help ease this fear. The one that sticks out the most is Psalm 17:8: *"Keep me as the apple of your eye; hide me in the shadow of your wings..."*

God is our perfect protector.

Scripture Reading: 2 Thessalonians 3:3

"But the Lord is faithful, and he will strengthen and protect you from the evil one."

Loneliness

Dear Lord,

Sometimes I don't feel your presence. Even after the most sacred day of the year, Easter, I feel lonely—not lonely for human company but for yours.

I know this is not your doing; it's mine. Your Word says, *"The LORD is near to all who call on him, to all who call to him in truth"* (Psalm 145:18).

Why do I allow inconsequential things to fill my mind and my time? Not bad things, just things that take over my mind and push you aside. I love it when our communion is open and honest, when I pour out my heart and you listen and fill my heart with song (Psalm 30:11-12).

I know our relationship is going right when I wake up in the morning and my mind and heart are already singing a song of praise before I even open my eyes. When that happens, I know: *"Surely you have granted him eternal blessings and made him glad with the joy of your presence"* (Psalm 21:6).

Lord, I don't choose to feel that self-made loneliness anymore. I choose you and your presence and your warm and loving companionship.

Shared from the Heart

Loneliness is a feeling that no one really wants. I hate it worse when I'm feeling lonely for the Lord. I only feel this way when I allow earthly things to come first over my time with him. He didn't move his presence from me; I backed away from him without even realizing it.

As I start putting my priorities back in place, I feel the loneliness fading away and the joy of a restored relationship filling my soul.

Scripture Reading: Exodus 33:14

"The LORD replied, My Presence will go with you, and I will give you rest."

Desert Wanderer

Dear Lord,

How many times have I read your Word and thought, "How in the world could the Israelites see and personally experience your miracles and provision and still turn their backs on you?" What were they thinking?

Then I take a look at my own life and see how many times I whined, grumbled, and turned my back on you. I'm afraid there has been a lot more times than I would like to admit. But through it all, you are my deliverer (Psalm 18:2), just like you were for the Israelites.

I have acted ungrateful, just like they did. I have wandered in my own desert many times but you always seem to "part the waters" for me and lead me to the other side.

Thank you for not just being the "deliverer" thousands of years ago but for still being in the "delivery" business today!

What a wonderful Savior you are. I don't deserve your unconditional love but, Lord, I do accept it!

Shared from the Heart

It's so much easier to see the frequent "mess-ups" of biblical people and think, "What does it take for someone to see the power of God? Were they blind?" Then the Holy Spirit reminds me of my many "blind" moments.

He also reminds me that just as God delivered his people many years ago, he will deliver his children today out of their own "desert wanderings."

Scripture Reading: Ephesians 2:4-5

"But because of his great love for us, God, who is rich in mercy, made us alive with Christ even when we were dead in transgressions—it is by grace you have been saved."

Argue or Trust?

Dear Lord,

In Exodus 3 and 4, I was reading about Moses arguing with you about why he couldn't go to Egypt to help free your people from slavery. He was feeling very inadequate and scared.

What do I argue with you about? "WHY would I argue with you?" is a better question. I know that you never ask me to do anything that you don't equip me to do. Am I missing out on great blessings because I don't trust you deeply enough? What has me so enslaved that I can't trust you or even myself? Do I dream too big and are they just "pipe dreams"? Where is the reality in them and where is my faith and trust in all this?

If I don't take a step in faith, and trust that you will certainly equip me, then you may take these dreams and let someone else accomplish them for your kingdom. Your work will be done one way or the other. I don't want to be wandering out in the desert while someone else accomplishes things that I should be doing.

Is it going to be me or someone else? Lord, let it be me!

Shared from the Heart

If we sincerely believe God is calling us to do something in particular for him, we cannot accomplish it if we don't trust him to equip us for the assignment.

He is not going to ask us to do something and then say, "Okay, you're on your own. See what you can do."

He will supply us with everything we need. All he needs from us is our obedience and childlike faith.

Scripture Reading: Matthew 17:20

"He replied, 'Because you have so little faith, I tell you the truth, if you have faith as small as a mustard seed, you can say to this mountain, "Move from here to there" and it will move. Nothing will be impossible for you.'"

Authority

Dear Lord,

When I tell you that I want you to be the "lord" over everything in my life but I hold back things for me to be "lord" over, am I just being "mouthy"? Where's the sincerity?

Am I placing a defiled offering on your altar like they did in Malachi 1? You deserve the very best from me—not perfection but my best. It takes a lot of effort to turn complete authority over to you but it is certainly not impossible because, with you, all things are possible (Matthew 19:26).

I also know, Lord, that this is not a one-time offering. I have to begin every day offering my life and authority to you. I know there will be days that I will give you authority just to take it back ten minutes later. The key is to keep giving it to you with a sincere and humble heart—a heart that places you on the throne and not me.

Shared from the Heart

I think giving authority over to the Lord every morning is a great way to start a day. However, there are days when we seem to be playing "ping pong." I give him authority, I take it back, I give him authority, and I take it back.

Letting someone else run your life is not easy but when it's the Lord, it's the right thing to do no matter how many times it takes.

Scripture Reading: Jude 24

"To him who is able to keep you from falling and to present you before his glorious presence without fault and with great joy—to the only God our Savior be glory, majesty, power and authority, through Jesus Christ our Lord before all ages, now and forevermore. Amen."

Unfailing Love

Dear Lord,

I love this season when Christians all over the world celebrate your birth.

I've got to admit that this time of the year I sometimes feel a little down and sort of lonely. I miss having someone to share with me all the things that go along with the holiday season. You know that I've always wanted to be loved like you see in the movies. I wanted someone to think I was the most beautiful and wonderful woman in all the world. I was going for that "love is blind" concept.

Then, as I sit here, I start to think about you and all you gave up to come to earth to live and die just for me. Why did you do that? I'm truly not worthy of such an expression of love, the kind of love John talks about in John 3:16. This kind of love, Lord, is just like you and no one else. No conditions, no reasons, no partiality—just plain and simple unfailing love, a love that endures forever (Jeremiah 31:3).

I love the way you love me. It's the best gift I could ever receive.

Shared from the Heart

There is only one person who can love us the way we truly need to be loved. The Lord loves us like no other and he's not too big or too macho to show it.

We can't do anything to earn this love; it's just there and it's just for us. The best thing of all is that it's unconditional, unfailing, and never-ending.

Scripture Reading: Isaiah 54:10

"Though the mountains be shaken and the hills be removed, yet my unfailing love for you will not be shaken nor my covenant of peace be removed says the LORD, who has compassion on you."

Morning Person

Dear Lord,

Praise you Lord, I have become a "morning" person. Not many years ago, people didn't even want to look my way until after 10:00 a.m. I could grumble and huff with the best. So, what happened?

I would have to say YOU happened. The more I took in your Word in the morning, the more I realized that being "grumpy" was not real Christ-like.

All through your Word, you talk about starting our morning with you. If it is important to you, it's important to me. Here are just a few scriptures that mention the morning and you:

- Isaiah 33:2—"*O LORD, be gracious to us; we long for you. Be our strength every morning, our salvation in time of distress.*"
- Psalm 90:14—"*Satisfy us in the morning with your unfailing love, that we may sing for joy and be glad all our days.*"
- Lamentations 3:22-23—"*Because of the LORD's great love we are not consumed, for his compassions never fail. They are new every morning; great is thy faithfulness.*"
- Mark 1:35—"*Very early in the morning, while it was still dark, Jesus got up, left the house and went off to a solitary place where he prayed.*"

You know what my day is going to be like and you also know that it's important for me to begin it with you, allowing you to "fill my soul with your fuel."

You, my Lord, have taken the grumpy out of my morning and replaced it with peace and joy. Only you can do that!

Shared from the Heart

I truly was not a "morning" person. I really didn't want to be talked to early in the morning and I certainly didn't like to hear that sweet voice that morning people seem to have. I needed time to get rid of the "grumpies" before I could face the day.

As I grew closer to the Lord, I realized that grumpiness was definitely not a "fruit of the spirit." I also realized that he is still in the miracle business. It took a while, but he helped me become someone that didn't scare people to death just because they spoke to me before 10:00 a.m.

Scripture Reading: Psalm 30:11-12

"You turned my wailing into dancing; you removed my sackcloth and clothed me with joy, that my heart may sing to you and not be silent. O LORD my God, I will give you thanks forever."

The True Lover of My Soul!

Dear Lord,

"Jesus, lover of my soul, Jesus, I will never let you go"…I love that song. I sing it over and over in my head. But how many times in one single day do I let you go? More than I want to count. The good news is that YOU never let me go. Nothing can separate us (Romans 8:39). You are not "wishy-washy" like me. You are strong, steadfast, and faithful. I'm so thankful for a God that is all-powerful, all-knowing, and all-loving.

I know there are times my decisions make you sad but they only make you sad because you know what's best for me and these "things" I chase after are not always for my good.

Through it all, you are there—my rock, my fortress, the "lover of my soul," and once again "*you pick me up from the miry clay and set my feet upon a rock*" (Psalm 40:2).

I can truly rely on you because you do love my soul; you gave your life for it.

Shared from the Heart

Isn't it great news that no matter how many times we let go of Jesus' hand, he's still holding on to ours? He never lets go and no matter how many times we fail, he will always pick us up and plant us upon a firm foundation. That foundation is Jesus. He is our rock and our only salvation.

Scripture Reading: 1 John 4:10

"This is love: not that we loved God, but that he loved us and sent his Son as an atoning sacrifice for our sins."

Experiences

Dear Lord,

Life is full of experiences—some good, some not so good. I wish I had had the faith and trust in you when I was younger that I have today. Some of those experiences would have turned out a little better.

As I reflect from this side, I really don't regret most of my "life experiences" because if I had not gone through them, I would not be able to help others who are facing the same thing. You have a way of putting people in our path who need to hear how we made it through what they might be experiencing today: someone who just lost a loved one and feels they cannot go on; someone who just found out their job has been eliminated and they don't know what to do now; someone who has a teenage daughter who is pregnant and they feel life is whirling out of control; someone who has been less than thrifty in spending and now finds themselves in financial trouble; or someone aging and the process scares them.

There are all kinds of experiences that people go through. Lord, help me not be afraid or too prideful to give an encouraging word and share what I know.

What I know is that there is absolutely nothing that we will go through that you are not mighty enough to get us to the other side of. That I have truly experienced.

Shared from the Heart

We will all go through many experiences during our lifetimes. I have found out that God will put people in your path who have been or are going through similar experiences to our own. When that happens, I believe that we need to share what we experienced and how God got us through.

Sometimes people just need to know that they are not alone and that there is a "light at the end of the tunnel"—and that the light is, of course, Jesus.

Scripture Reading: Romans 12:6-8

"We have different gifts, according to the grace given us. If a man's gift is prophesying, let him use it in proportion to his faith. If it is serving, let him serve; if it is teaching, let him teach; if it is encouraging, let him encourage; if it is contributing to the needs of others, let him give generously; if it is leadership, let him govern diligently; if it is showing mercy, let him do it cheerfully."

Finer Things in Life

Dear Lord,

I sit here sometimes and think about things I don't have and, at my age, will probably never have. I will never have a huge, fancy mansion, decorated by an interior designer; I will never drive a Rolls Royce; and I will probably never wear designer originals.

NEVER, until I get to heaven. What a wonderful thought. Never is not really never. I can just hear you saying, "Not on this earth, my daughter, but just wait and see what I have stored up for you when you get here. I have a place prepared just for you. What you will be wearing is beyond the imagination of any designer and everything was prepared with you in mind."

So, Lord, I'm just going to relax on this earth and not worry about all the "stuff" I don't have. Instead, I'm going to anticipate with great joy what wonderful surprises you, the "Master Designer," have in store for me, one of your "designer originals," one day when I get to heaven.

Shared from the Heart

My family and I like to tour what we call mansions. We like to see "how the other side lives." This can be fun but sometimes it can be a little depressing.

More than likely, I will never live in a mansion on earth but, oh, wait until I get to heaven. There is no way my little brain can imagine how beautiful and wonderful it will be. It will be worth the wait!

Scripture Reading: Revelation 21:1-4

"Then I saw a new heaven and a new earth, for the first heaven and the first earth had passed away and there was no longer any sea. I saw the Holy City, the new Jerusalem, coming down out of heaven from God, prepared as a bride beautifully dressed for her husband. And I heard a loud voice from the throne saying, 'Now the dwelling of God is with men and he will live with them and be their God. He will wipe every tear from their eyes. There will be no more death or mourning or crying or pain, for the old order of things has passed away.'"

july 10, 2017

Commitment

Dear Lord,

You know I committed my life to you many, many years ago. However, through our journey together, I walked away from you for a season but returned and now my life is totally yours. But, as all humans do, I find myself leaning a little on the "me" side and a little less on the "Lord" side at times. I hate it when I do that.

What I want, Lord, is to be wholly and completely committed to you. When you look on earth as you did in 2 Chronicles 16:9: "*For the eyes of the LORD range throughout the earth to strengthen those whose hearts are fully committed to him*", I want you to see my heart as a heart "fully committed."

Commitment is part of loving someone. If I truly love you, I will be committed to you.

I want to start every day with a statement of commitment giving you authority over the day. I will need your strength and your power to do this but as you have promised, your strength is mine (Isaiah 41:10).

Shared from the Heart

Don't you wish that when the Lord looks in everyone's heart on earth and when he looks at yours, he will see a totally committed heart? No leaning a little to the left or right—just a pure heart. I do.

The only leaning I want him to see is me leaning on him.

Scripture Reading: Numbers 30:2

"When a man makes a vow to the LORD or takes an oath to obligate himself by a pledge, he must not break his word but must do everything he said."

Isaiah 41:10 NIV
NLT

"Don't be afraid, for I am with you. Don't be discouraged, for I am your God. I will strengthen you and help you. I will hold you up in my victorious right hand."

july 12, 2017

Just for Me

Dear Lord,

As I read, once again, the first part of the Easter story, I saw something I don't believe ever stood out to me before. When you were on the cross and said, "*Father, forgive them for they do not know what they are doing*" (Luke 23:34), in my heart I believe you were not just talking about the people of that day; you were talking about me, too.

I was just thinking about what we mean when we say, "I have a personal relationship with Jesus" or "He is my personal Savior." How more personal can you get than what you did for me? You gave up everything and came to a place where you would be mocked and ridiculed, and eventually killed.

Because of what you gave up for me—yes, for me—I can have a relationship with the one true God, Creator of everything, YOU. You built a bridge for me to cross over with your shed blood, your death, and—praise God—your resurrection.

Shared from the Heart

Have you ever thought about your "personal relationship" with the Lord? Just how personal is it? He gave up everything for you and me so why are we not willing to lay everything out there for him?

To have a real personal relationship, you have to be completely open and honest—no unrepentant sins or regrets. He knows them anyway. He likes to be personal, too, and has a "personal" forgiveness ready just for us. All we have to do is ask for it.

Scripture Reading: John 20:29

"Then Jesus told him, 'Because you have seen me, you have believed; blessed are those who have not seen and yet have believed.'"

Loving Others

Dear Lord,

It's so easy for me to look around and see how other people should lead their lives. How easy it is to see other people's shortcomings. Then, with tender love, you show me mine. You tell me to do my best, to show others my excitement for you and the things that have eternal purpose. You actually show me that I'm not "perfect," except in Christ.

It's my job or responsibility to love others, be a good example to others, and always be prepared to share what you have done for me (1 Peter 3:15).

I want you, Lord, to be patient and gentle with me. Why should I act any other way to others? As you use all your attributes listed in Colossians 3:12 on me, help me to do the same with others.

Shared from the Heart

There are times I don't feel like being loving, compassionate, kind, humble, gentle, or patient with others. To be honest, I just want them to "go away and leave me alone."

I've got to say that I'm really thankful the Lord doesn't treat me like that. Where in the world would I be if he weren't loving, compassionate, kind, humble, gentle, and, most of all, patient with me? I would be in a heap of trouble, that's for sure!

If I'm going to be a Christ-like example, I don't have a choice. I have to allow all of these attributes to show through me, no matter if I want to at the moment or not.

Scripture Reading: Colossians 3:12

"As God's chosen people, holy and dearly loved, clothe yourselves with compassion, kindness, humility, gentleness and patience."

Wasted Time

Dear Lord,

I don't understand why, time after time, I find myself sitting around "channel surfing." Relaxing and watching TV after a hard day at work is not wrong but allowing it to consume all my time is.

There are things, Lord, I could be doing that take less time than sitting "comatose" in front of my TV. I could be calling someone whom I know could use a kind word; I could be sending someone an encouraging note (that's always nice to receive). Those are just a couple of things that could have eternal value. This is what my life should be about.

You tell me in your Word to "*store up for yourself treasures in heaven. For where your treasure is, there your heart will be also*" (Matthew 6:20-21). Sitting in front of a TV twenty-four/seven does not have much eternal value, especially with what's on TV these days.

I know there needs to be a good balance between ministering to others and relaxing. I'm depending on you, Lord, to help me find that balance and stay with it.

Shared from the Heart

I don't know about you but I struggle with "balance" a lot. I put myself on a guilt trip thinking things like, "I'm watching too much TV; I need to be feeding the poor" or "I'm reading too much; I need to be out witnessing." How about, "I'm spending too much time having fun; I need to be studying my Bible"?

All these things are good and we should definitely be doing them but it all boils down to "godly balance." God wants us to enjoy our lives but he also expects us to put him above all.

Scripture Reading: Proverbs 3:5-8

"Trust in the LORD with all your heart and lean not on your own understanding; in all your ways acknowledge him, and he will make your paths straight. Do not be wise in your own eyes, fear the LORD and shun evil. This will bring health to your body and nourishment to your bones."

Shout from the Rooftop!

Dear Lord,

How can I say that I love you and fail to share with others what you have done for me in the past, present, and what you have promised to do for me in the future?

Just like you did for the people of Israel, you do for me. You brought me back when I wandered off; you comfort me when I mourn (Matthew 5:4); you rejoice with me during times of rejoicing and protect me under the shadow of your wings (Psalm 36:7).

Why do I just continue to let you provide for me and not tell others about it? I should be telling others every day, "Do you know what the Lord has done for me?"

I love you for who you are and I will shout from the rooftops what an amazing God you are to me!

Shared from the Heart

My gift is not "stand-on-the-street" evangelism. I lean quite heavily on "lifestyle" evangelism.

Sometimes that can be a cop-out. How can I accept all the wonderful things that God does for me and not share it with anyone who will listen? The Bible doesn't really tell us to be timid in our witnessing but it does tell us to speak God's Word with great boldness.

Scripture Reading: Zephaniah 3:17

"The LORD your God is with you, he is mighty to save. He will take delight in you, he will quiet you with his love, he will rejoice over you with singing."

Just Because

Dear Lord,

Why did you give up your life and suffer so much pain just because you love me?

Why do you always forgive my pride, my self-centeredness, and all that other rotten stuff I allow in my life just because you love me?

Why do you cover me with your wings of protection just because you love me?

Why do you discipline me just because you love me?

Why do you fill me with your wonderful peace when there's nothing but chaos going on around me just because you love me?

1 John 4:16 says: "*God is love.*" You can't help yourself from loving and taking care of your children; that's just who you are and what you are all about—love.

Hallelujah, praise the Lord, and amen. So it is "just because you love me"!

Shared from the Heart

The answer to many questions is so simple sometimes that it becomes hard for us to grasp. Why does God do all the things he does for us? Simple answer: he loves us.

The hard part is understanding and accepting this "unconditional" love. Everything God does is out of his love for his children.

Mind-boggling, isn't it?

Scripture Reading: Psalm 103:13

"As a father has compassion on his children, so the LORD has compassion on those who fear him."

Holding Hands

Dear Lord,

I love it when you minister to me in such a personal way. You take a verse from your Word that you know I love and cherish and you show me something new and exciting.

Isaiah 41:13 says this: "*For I am the LORD your God who takes hold of your right hand and says to you, do not fear, I will help you.*" I love that: you holding my right hand—very comforting. But then you showed me Isaiah 41:10: "*So do not fear, for I am with you; do not be dismayed, for I am your God. I will strengthen you and help you; I will uphold you with my righteous right hand.*"

Now, Lord, I'm getting a whole different picture. Instead of walking side by side with me, holding my right hand, you have my right hand in your right hand. This means to me that you are standing before me, clasping my right hand with yours and leading the way for me—every step of the way. Whatever starts to hit me hits you; whatever tries to overcome me has to deal with you first. You are not surprised by what comes my way, nor are you ever caught off-guard. You are always there, holding my right hand. It doesn't matter if you are beside me, in front of me, or behind me; you are there because you promised.

Please don't ever let me let go of your hand! What a place of comfort and security.

Shared from the Heart

For me, holding hands is very personal. I don't usually go around holding just anyone's hand. Now, picture God holding your hand in his. Doesn't that give you goose bumps? Just think about the Creator of the entire universe holding your hand.

That proves to me that he is not some far-off god way up in the sky but he is a loving, tender God that knows when we need it and reaches down and holds our hand. That, my friend, is very powerful.

Scripture Reading: Psalm 16:8

"I have set the LORD always before me. Because he is at my right hand, I will not be shaken."

More than Enough

Dear Lord,

"All I have in you is more than enough for me." That's a sentence from a song that I woke up with on my mind this morning. It's also going to be my theme today. Whatever happens today, you are more than enough for me.

Family may let me down, work might seem more than I can handle, aches and pains of this body may appear but "all I have in you is more than enough for me."

Lord, if you are truly "more than enough for me," the desires of my heart will be the same as your desires for me. Psalm 37:4 says: "*Delight yourself in the LORD and He will give you the desires of your heart.*" You are all I want and you are the desire of my heart.

Shared from the Heart

I love waking up with a "Jesus" song on my mind and making it a "theme" song for the day—for example, the song "More than Enough." Whatever circumstances the day brings, we can rely on our faithful, reliable God to see us through. He can be our sufficiency.

He definitely is "all we need."

Scripture Reading: Psalm 92:1-2

"It is good to praise the LORD and make music to your name, O Most High, to proclaim your love in the morning, and your faithfulness at night."

Good Representative

Dear Lord,

As your child, I should represent your qualities. But do I? Do I show others kindness, goodness, and self-control? Do I allow you to fill me with the fruit of your spirit (Galatians 5:22)? Am I reflecting your love to all and not just to a chosen few? How about patience? Am I patient with people who tend to irritate me more easily than others?

Do people see me as a faithful person or unstable in my faith and in my promises that I make?

Lord, I want to be a good representative of you. I want people to see your perfect qualities when they look at me. I want them to see my good character, my integrity, my peace, my joy, and my Savior.

Shared from the Heart

I think if there is one virtue I need to work on most, it would have to be patience, especially while driving. I can be driving along praying, singing along with worship music, enjoying my time with the Lord and then, wham, someone darts in front of me when there's no room for me and him, too. I catch myself saying things that are certainly not representative of the way Jesus would act or talk.

Of course, these people have no idea I just "lost it" with them but Jesus does. That fact should bring me to my knees and make me try to be a better example of love, patience, and, yes, self-control (especially since I have a fish emblem on my bumper).

Scripture Reading: 1 Timothy 4:12

"Set an example for the believers in speech, in life, in love, in faith and in purity."

My Own Worst Enemy

Dear Lord,

When I'm in great distress, like right now, I become my own worst enemy. I'm not only hurting but I feel all alone. I feel unworthy of your love, of your protection, and of your provision. I wonder why you would ever deliver me or answer my prayers. I feel hopeless.

Boy, I'm glad I don't feel this way a lot. It's a real downer!

One thing I know for sure, Lord, is that I can put myself down as much as I want but you never do. While I'm putting myself down, you are lifting me up.

You lift me, you minister to me, you rejoice in me, and you sing over me (Zephaniah 3:17). I am truly never alone—maybe lonely, but never alone.

Shared from the Heart

Sometimes I just beat myself into the ground. I'm not sure why but I work myself into feeling totally unwanted and unworthy. I do believe that is where Satan wants believers to be because, in that place, we are not very usable.

If you ever find yourself there, don't allow yourself to stay there. Remember, God loves lifting us up and he rejoices and sings over us.

Scripture Reading: Psalm 40:1-3

"I waited patiently for the LORD; he turned to me and heard my cry. He lifted me out of the slimy pit, out of the mud and mire; he set my feet on a rock and gave me a firm place to stand. He put a new song in my mouth, a hymn of praise to our God. Many will see and fear and put their trust in the LORD."

Nearness

Dear Lord,

Sitting and watching my sister struggle just to breathe is absolutely heartbreaking. I feel so helpless. If I could breathe for her, I would. Lord, she needs your touch.

As I write this letter to you, a song is playing on the radio: "Oh God Be Near." Right now that's all I ask. Lord, just be near. With your nearness, we will not be consumed. You will get us through this because you are faithful. You are always there no matter what.

God, just be near!

Shared from the Heart

In the worst of times, all we really need is to feel God's presence and to remember his beautiful promises—his promises that he will always be with us and his promise that if we draw near to him, he will draw near to us.

He truly wants to be in our presence.

Scripture Reading: Psalm 145:18

"The LORD is near to all who call on him, to all who call on him in truth."

Attributes of Love

Dear Lord,

How like you to leave me instructions on how to love. Who can instruct better than the one who created love and us to love?

When I do things for others in the name of love, what is my motivation? Do I have ulterior motives or a secret agenda? Loving and caring for others should spill out from my love for you. My motive should be to please the one that loves me more than life itself, and you proved that love on the cross.

Love is patient and kind and all the other things 1 Corinthians 13 says it is. Lord, I so want to love like that.

Please fill me with a love for others that will only reflect one thing—YOU.

Shared from the Heart

Have you ever thought about how it would be to love and not expect something in return?

Am I capable of loving a clerk at the store who was less than friendly for no apparent reason? Or how about the person who would not let you on the freeway even when you were just about to run out of room to get on? Or maybe that person who caused you great pain in your life?

I believe we should love with an unconditional love—a love like Jesus has for us.

Scripture Reading: 1 Corinthians 13:4-8a

"Love is patient, love is kind, it does not envy, it does not boast, it is not proud. It is not rude, it is not self-seeking, it is not easily angered, it keeps no record of wrongs. Love does not delight in evil but rejoices with the truth. It always protects, always trusts, always hopes, always perseveres. Love never fails."

Ministering Music

Dear Lord,

There are times I have no energy, no enthusiasm, and no earthly desire to move. I feel "stuck" to my chair. How do I get up and get going?

I love it when you use music to minister to me. As I am feeling less than energetic, a verse to a song comes to my mind that lifts me: "Turn your eyes upon Jesus, look full in his wonderful face and the things of this earth will grow strangely dim in the light of his glory and grace." Wow! That should do it.

After I turn my eyes upon you, you tell me in another song (and also a Bible verse), "Cast all your cares upon Jesus, He is truly able, so just leave them there, cast all your cares upon him" (1 Peter 5:7).

Okay, now I've turned my eyes to you, I've cast all my cares upon you, but why? Another song answers that question: "Because He lives, I can face tomorrow, because He lives, all fear is gone. Because I know He holds the future and life is worth the living just because He lives." Praise you, Lord; because you live, I can do anything.

One last song: "God is good all the time and all the time God is good."

Shared from the Heart

God uses music to minister to me all the time. He knows I can get lost in a song. Many songwriters go to God's Word for inspiration. It's fun to be reading scripture and realize that there's been a song written from that particular scripture.

One that comes to my mind is called "Psalm 40" by Newsong. It goes like this:

I waited patiently for the Lord;
He turned to me and heard my cry.
He lifted me out of the slimy pit,
Out of the mud and mire;
He set my feet on a rock
And gave me a firm place to stand.
He put a new song in my mouth,
A hymn of praise to our God.
Many will see and fear the Lord
And put their trust in him.

Scripture Reading: Psalm 9:1-2

"I will praise you, O LORD, with all my heart; I will tell of all your wonders. I will be glad and rejoice in you; I will sing praise to your name, O Most High."

Your Presence

Dear Lord,

No matter my thoughts, words, or deeds, your love and presence are always there. You do not change. You are not like me—high on life one day and the very next day feeling like a failure and not knowing what to do next.

What you do is very amazing. You ride my ups and downs with me every inch of the way, always loving, always encouraging, always guiding.

Your presence in my life is your greatest gift to me and I thank you for it.

Shared from the Heart

Can you imagine being without God's presence in your life? How empty that must feel. As believers, we don't have to worry about that because he lives in us.

Sometimes because of the way we are acting, we don't want to acknowledge his presence but he is there nonetheless.

Scripture Reading: Isaiah 43:2-3

"When you pass through the waters, I will be with you; and when you pass through the rivers, they will not sweep over you. When you walk through the fire, you will not be burned; the flames will not set you ablaze. For I am the LORD, your God, the Holy One of Israel, your Savior."

Gifts

Dear Lord,

I am learning, Lord, that you "gift" us in different ways. We don't all have the same gifts.

Thank you for showing me in your Word that "*We are the clay, you are the potter; we are the work of your hand*" (Isaiah 64:8). You made us all different for a reason. All I need to do is be the best I can be with the strengths and weaknesses you have given me. With my faith in you, I can accomplish the things you have purposed me to do.

You have a lot of things you need done before your return and it's going to take all of us and our different gifts, talents, and desires to get it done.

I want to be what YOU want me to be.

Shared from the Heart

I once went through a Bible study called "Experiencing God." It is a great study. One of the things I learned was that when you see God working, you should join him.

I believe there are things to be done around us that we need to do that call for gifts we may not possess or excel in, like working in Vacation Bible School. We might not be gifted to teach a class but just about anyone can serve refreshments or just smile and show God's love to precious children.

It takes all of us working together, using all our gifts, to accomplish God's plan.

Scripture Reading: 1 Peter 4:10

"Each one should use whatever gift he has received to serve others, faithfully, administering God's grace in its various forms."

Closed Doors

Dear Lord,

When I've exhausted all of my ideas of what to do next, where do I turn? When all the doors I try to open are closed, what do I do? Do I take "closed" doors as the answer and just give up? Good questions, but what are the answers?

I know with all my heart your Word has the answers to all these questions. Show me, Lord. Show me in your Word where to go, what to do next.

Jeremiah 29:13 says, "*You will seek me and find me when you seek me with all your heart.*" Isn't that what I've been doing? If it isn't, show me the error of my ways. Help me to seek you with all my heart, soul, mind, and strength. You said we will find you and when we do, you will bring us back from captivity.

Show me, Lord, which way to go.

Shared from the Heart

I do not believe that giving up is the right answer when we run into what appears to be a closed door. I do believe when we seek him with all our hearts and stop long enough to hear his still small voice, he will show us which door to go through and when.

Scripture Reading: Jeremiah 6:16

"This is what the LORD says: Stand at the crossroads and look; ask for the ancient paths, ask where the good way is and walk in it, and you will find rest for your souls."

Slavery

Dear Lord,

As I studied your Word this morning in Joshua 5, I see where you gave the children of Israel hope and a future when you led them out of Egypt. You promised them a land flowing with "milk and honey" but because of their choices (grumbling and no deep trust in you), they were not blessed with seeing this new land but their children were.

You said, "*Today, I have rolled away the reproach of Egypt from you…*" (Joshua 5:9).

What has had me enslaved that you have set me free from? I don't even have to think twice; I know right off what it is. It's that certain period of time in my past that I'm not proud of and have a hard time letting go of. But, once and for all, I can see and feel your deliverance.

I can now enter into your "promised land," which is a land of self-respect and forgiveness. I'm not going to let my past "enslave" me any longer. You have broken my chains of slavery.

Shared from the Heart

God has set me free from a lot of strongholds in my life. Because I have a tendency to beat myself up, I have asked for freedom from the same thing several times.

I forget sometimes that once he forgives and sets me free, he forgets. I'm the one who keeps bringing it up and can't let it go.

When he forgives, he's done with it…and so should I be.

Scripture Reading: Romans 6:22

"But now that you have been set free from sin and have become slaves to God, the benefit you reap leads to holiness and the result is eternal life."

El Shaddi

Dear Lord,

I love your different names and what they mean. I want to share with you what they mean to me personally.

Today let's take El Shaddi, All-Sufficient One. It has taken me a very long time to fully understand and believe that meaning. Time after time you have shown me that you are all I need. I know now that nothing else really matters but my relationship with you. You are more than sufficient.

When I'm living like the only thing that is important is our relationship, my other relationships are what they should be. I will be the mother, mother-in-law, grandmother, sister, aunt, co-worker, friend, and fellow believer I should be.

Without you, I have nothing. With you, I have everything!

I love you, my "All-Sufficient One."

Shared from the Heart

Wouldn't life be easier if we could just accept the fact that God is really all we need? He is the "all-sufficient one."

With him, we can be truly satisfied.

Scripture Reading: Psalm 107:8-9

"Let them give thanks to the LORD for his unfailing love and his wonderful deeds for men, for he satisfies the thirsty and fills the hungry with good things."

Elohim

Dear Lord,

Elohim means Creator. When I started thinking about what that really means, I was surprised. Yes, you created everything and I know and believe that with all my heart, but what surprises me is that not everyone believes that way. How sad is that? I knew that but I really didn't give a lot of thought to it before.

I love looking at all your beautiful creation: the sky, the stars, the mountains, the gorgeous flowers. I feel sorry for those who look at these things and think that they "just happened" and they aren't able to feel the gratitude to the One that actually "made them happen." You spoke and so it was.

Who wants to believe that we "just happened" instead of believing a wonderful Creator "*knit me together in my mother's womb*" (Psalm 139:13)? You wanted me here and here I am.

I'm not here by accident. I'm here because you have a plan and a purpose for me. You created me for a reason. That is very cool!

Shared from the Heart

I love believing in my Creator. I also love knowing that the God of the universe saw fit to bring me into this world and laid out plans just for me.

Yes, I messed up those plans at times but he loved me so much he forgave me my mess-ups and put me back where he wanted me to be now. That is a personal Creator, not a "boom" and there you are!

Scripture Reading: Psalm 102:25

"In the beginning you laid the foundations of the earth, and the heavens are the work of your hands."

Adonai

Dear Lord,

Adonai means Lord and Master. This one means a lot to me now. When I was first saved many, many years ago, you became my Savior. As I have matured spiritually over the years, you have become my "Lord and Master." I wish I had crowned you that way back when and the decisions I made would have been a little bit different.

All I can say now is that I truly desire your lordship in all areas of my life. It's a daily struggle because I like to be my own boss but I have learned that my being the boss is not the best way. Your way is best—not always the easiest, but always the best.

You are truly my sweet Adonai.

Shared from the Heart

You know, God is either our Master or he's not. We can't divide our devotion. Either we are fully in or we're out.

I tried to ride the fence too many years trying to have two masters. It doesn't work. Jesus doesn't want part of us. Jesus wants all of us.

Scripture Reading: Colossians 1:10

"And we pray this in order that you may live a life worthy of the Lord and may please him in every way; bearing fruit in every good work, growing in the knowledge of God."

Jehovah-rapha

Dear Lord,

Your name today is Jehovah-rapha, Lord Who Heals. Since I am home sick today, this name is totally appropriate. I do need healing; being sick is not fun.

As I think about the deeper meaning of the Lord Who Heals, I can see so much more. You have healed me in so many ways: physically, emotionally, and relationally.

You healed my broken heart several times and in ways no one else could ever do. You healed my broken spirit when it got trampled and stepped on. The longer I live, the more you heal. You not only heal things in my present but you can take "long-ago" situations and bring present-day healing.

Where would I be if you were not my Jehovah-rapha? I do not wish to find out!

Shared from the Heart

Have you ever prayed for healing for someone or even yourself but that healing did not come? I'm sure we all have at some time. I know God can heal any time he wants to but there are times he chooses not to. That will definitely be one of my questions for him when I get to heaven but, until then, I choose to trust his heart and his faithfulness.

I will praise him and claim him as my Jehovah-rapha.

Scripture Reading: Jeremiah 17:14

"Heal me, O LORD, and I will be healed; save me and I will be saved, for you are the one I praise."

Living Water

Dear Lord,

When my mouth gets so dry that it actually sticks together (yuck), the only thing that will quench that thirst is ice cold water.

When my soul gets thirsty, the only thing that can quench that thirst is your "living water" and the only supplier of this water is you.

You tell me in John 7:38 that this "living water" is mine just for the asking. I also know, as I am a believer, that you live inside me, so I do not ever have to be thirsty again (spiritually speaking).

You and I both know, Lord, that there have been times when I didn't drink your water. I withdrew and went a different direction, for a season, and allowed my soul to become parched.

Praise be to God that your Word and your promises are true! You are a bottomless fountain of "living water," always there and always willing to quench my thirsty soul.

The only thirst I ever want to have again is a deep and abiding thirst for you.

Shared from the Heart

Drought can bring havoc to your lawn, your flowers, and everything else that needs water for life and for growth.

There is another type of drought that can bring havoc to our lives. That is "spiritual" drought. When we allow the things of this world to fill us, we are missing out on the bountiful springs of living water that only Jesus can provide.

Scripture Reading: John 4:13-14

"Jesus answered, 'Everyone who drinks this water will be thirsty again, but whoever drinks the water I give him will never thirst. Indeed, the water I give him will become in him a spring of water welling up to eternal life.'"

Victory

Dear Lord,

Here I go again with a song, my favorite old hymn: "Victory in Jesus, my Savior, forever. He sought me and bought me with His redeeming blood; He loved me ere I knew Him and all my love is due Him, He plunged me to victory, beneath the cleansing flood."

Oh, how I love that song. Oh, how I love all the sweet victories you bring into my life, especially the big one that you just handed over to me. All I did was confess to you this "lifetime" habit had to go and you removed it. I know that some victories have to be worked out a little more but then there are times you allow me the privilege of seeing your mighty work in a way that allows for no doubt in my life at all—no doubt that you have all the power and all the might, no doubt that you love me, and no doubt that you live in me.

Yes, I truly have "Victory in Jesus."

Shared from the Heart

How sweet victory is when you recognize just who gave it to you. Overcoming a stronghold in your own power is short-lived. Overcoming a stronghold through the power of the Holy Spirit is truly a victory.

Scripture Reading: 1 John 5:4-5

"For everyone born of God overcomes the world. This is the victory that has overcome the world, even our faith. Who is it that overcomes the world? Only he who believes that Jesus is the Son of God."

Jehovah-shalom

Dear Lord,

Your name today is Jehovah-shalom, Lord of Peace. I love this name for you because that is what you have been time and time again to me—not peace like the world talks about, but the calming, deep peace that only comes from you. It's a peace that cannot be totally described but a peace that reassures me of your presence.

Peace during times when everything in me thinks that life, as I know it, is over. Peace during a time of deep, heartbreaking loss through the death of a loved one. Peace when changes in your life take place and you are nowhere near ready for them. Romans 8:6 says: "*The mind controlled by the Spirit is life and peace*"—that is real peace.

Yes, Lord, you are truly my Jehovah-shalom.

Shared from the Heart

Unless you have experienced it, it's hard to understand how you can feel a deep, calming peace when everything in your life seems to be falling apart.

This kind of peace is only available when you are holding on to God's hand with all the strength and power you possess.

Scripture Reading: Psalm 85:8

"I will listen to what God the LORD will say; he promises peace to his people, his saints—but let them not return to folly."

Strongholds

Dear Lord,

Strongholds that I've allowed in my life have kept our relationship from being all you want it to be. Thank you for showing me that I have allowed my heart's desire to be something other than you.

There's nothing, Lord, any sweeter than an intimate relationship with you that is pure and sincere, coming from a heart that has emptied itself of "self" and allowed you to fill it with "you."

True freedom is searching my soul and acknowledging that there are things in my life that need to be handed over to you.

It's not easy but giving up strongholds that have become a part of me brings such wonderful cleansing that I'm not sure what took me so long to give them up. Deliverance is not "magic," but right at this moment it almost feels like it!

Shared from the Heart

It's hard to understand how we can let something get such a hold on us that we don't believe it's possible to let go of it. Trust me, I have found out through experience that there is nothing too big or too strong for our God to defeat.

Give him a chance; he loves to show his muscles!

Scripture Reading: Psalm 32:7

"You are my hiding place; you will protect me from trouble and surround me with songs of deliverance."

Jehovah-raah

Dear Lord,

Today you are my Jehovah-raah, My Shepherd. How many times in my life have you had to come and get this little "sheep," turn her around, and bring her back to your pasture? More times than I can recall. Why on earth do I do that? I guess I forgot how good it feels to be safely abiding within your fold.

I think I wander off sometimes and don't even realize I'm doing it until I feel the Holy Spirit taking me by my shoulders and turning me around, telling me, "You really don't want to go this way; follow me."

I love the fact that you don't just leave your sheep out there to wander around forever. Sheep are pretty dumb animals so I doubt if they would come back on their own. But you, Lord, will guide, protect, and discipline, when necessary, until they are safely home.

What a loving Shepherd you are. I love being one of your sheep.

Shared from the Heart

Where in the world would we be without the Holy Spirit's nudging, guidance, and conscience reminder? I know where I'd be and the thought makes me shudder.

Of course, we can have all the nudging, guidance, and conscience reminder in the world but if we don't take heed and obey, it doesn't do us any good.

Be obedient—stay in the fold.

Scripture Reading: Psalm 37:23

"Commit your way to the LORD; trust in him."

Holy

Dear Lord,

Why is it I try to be holier on Sunday than on any other day? For instance, what I catch myself watching on TV during the week, I won't watch on Sunday. It's great that Sundays are so special to me but it really doesn't make a lot of sense. I'm called to be holy all the time, not just on Sunday. 1 Peter 1:15-16 says, "*Just as he who called us is holy, so be holy in all you do; for it is written: Be holy, because I am holy.*"

You are not asking me to be "perfect." You are telling me to be holy. The only thing that makes me holy is the blood of Jesus. Since I am covered with your blood, I should want to be like you: "Christ-like."

You are holy and I will strive to be holy in everything I do, Sunday through Saturday.

Shared from the Heart

As believers, we should be striving all of our days to be holy. This sounds like an enormous task but it can be done.

If we are living in God's will, discussing all decisions with him, reading his Word, and obeying his commands, we are striving for holiness. Not perfection, just plain ol' holiness.

Scripture Reading: 2 Corinthians 7:2

"Since we have these promises, dear friends, let us purify ourselves from everything that contaminates body and spirit, perfecting holiness out of reverence for God."

My Life Song

Dear Lord,

There's a song that says, "Let my life song sing to you." What is my life song singing?

Through the years, my life has sung many different tunes:

- It sang "rock and roll" in my early years after I first found you. I was ready to rock this world for you but instead I started rolling with it.
- It sang the "blues" during great losses of loved ones and broken relationships.
- It sang "hard rock" as I went back and forth with our relationship, causing myself a lot of hard, rocky times.
- It sang "opera" when I was "high" on life and everything seemed to be going my way.
- It sang a "lullaby" during my motherhood and grandmother stages.

What is it singing now? I hope my "life song" is showing you pure adoration and love and is singing the "gospel" of the good news for everyone to see.

Shared from the Heart

When I look back at my life, I see a lot of "ups and downs," "highs and lows." There's a song that, for me, brings it all together. The chorus goes like this:

> When we all get to heaven,
> What a day of rejoicing that will be!
> When we all see Jesus
> We'll sing and shout the victory!

Scripture Reading: Psalm 100:2

"Worship the LORD with gladness; come before him with joyful songs."

Praise

Dear Lord,

What exactly is praise? I can only answer for myself and to me praise is thanking you for what you have done for me but also thanking you for allowing me to see you and know you.

I don't think I praise you enough; in fact, I'm sure I don't.

Lord, I just want to tell you of a few things that I praise you for:

- For being, as a song puts it, "bigger than the air I breathe."
- For giving up everything and becoming a human like me but without sin.
- For setting up a plan that would reconcile the world back to you.
- For following through with that plan and laying down your life for me.
- For showing me your power by not staying in the grave but being victorious over it.
- For all your promises in your Word, promises that you have always been faithful to keep and always will be.
- For loving me enough to save me, guide me, and keep me on the right path no matter how many times I try to veer to the right or left of it.

I will praise you today, I will praise you tomorrow, and I will praise you through all of eternity!

Shared from the Heart

When I was much younger, I remember thinking, "All we're going to do in heaven is sit around and sing praises forever? That could get a little boring."

I was quite young and immature with that thought.

We will be doing a lot more than that but if that's all we did, I'm all in! There's no way I could sing enough praises to my God and Savior. I now love the thought of singing praises throughout eternity.

Scripture Reading: Isaiah 61:10

"I delight greatly in the LORD; my soul rejoices in my God. For he has clothed me with garments of salvation and arrayed me in a robe of righteousness, as a bridegroom adorns his head like a priest, and as a bride adorns herself with her jewels."

El Roi

Dear Lord,

Why do I think I can get something by you? You are El Roi, God Who Sees All.

My heart knows you see all but intellectually I think I try to "pull something over" on you. Surely I'm not that dumb! There are times I try not to think so much about what I'm doing and then I guess I think it sneaks by you. I don't admit it so you don't see it. What kind of thinking is that?

I do know one thing: you are El Roi, God Who Sees All. It doesn't matter if I admit it or not—you still see it. I know one other thing: you love it when I'm totally open and honest with you. That allows you to do your wonderful cleansing and there's nothing like a deep-down spiritual cleansing from you.

Thank you for "seeing all" and yet still loving me!

Shared from the Heart

There's nothing better than having an "open and honest" relationship with the Lord. On the other side of the coin, when I'm doing something that I don't want to talk to him about, that's a problem. He already knows what's going on so why hold back and act like I'm getting away with something?

God sees all but there is nothing that will keep him from loving us anyway.

Scripture Reading: Psalm 32:5

"I acknowledged my sin to you and did not cover up my iniquity. I said, 'I will confess my transgressions to the LORD'—and you forgave the guilt of my sin."

Sometimes

Dear Lord,

When all is well and life is good, do I have a tendency to draw away from you like the Israelites did? Do I get a "false" sense of security and think I can make it on my own? I would like to say no to these questions but in all honesty I would have to say, "sometimes."

When everything is "rosy," there may be times when I don't let you permeate my thoughts, but let a problem and/or fear enter into the picture and the first one I think of is you. I'm truly sorry I handle things that way. You should be my first thought no matter what is happening in my life.

Boy, you and I have a lot to work on in me and I guess we will be doing that until you return or call me home.

Thanks for never giving up on me.

Shared from the Heart

I've heard this phrase and have even used it myself many times: "I just give up." It's a pretty sad sentence. I'm very glad God never uses those words on his children even when he sees us trying to handle things on our own time and time again.

He won't give up because we belong to him and we are very important. He began a good work in us and he won't stop until it's completed.

Scripture Reading: Psalm 100:5

"For the LORD is good and his love endures forever; his faithfulness continues through all generations."

Spirit and Truth

Dear Lord,

For some reason, the phrase "in spirit and in truth" has been on my mind a lot lately.

This phrase reminds me that my worship should be "in spirit and in truth." So what does that mean? To me, it reminds me that my corporate worship time is for an audience of ONE, no awareness of anyone else around. It also reminds me that I must be open and honest, straight from the heart. When I lift up prayers to you, they should always be my honest, heartfelt requests, not wordy, flowery prayers—just prayers from my heart, "in spirit and in truth."

When it's all said and done, I want my life to reflect a life lived "in spirit and in truth," just your spirit and just your truth.

Shared from the Heart

When I first think of worship, I think of corporate worship at church. Worship is not just what we do on Sundays. Worship goes much deeper than that. It's how we should live our lives. We should be in a constant "worship" mode with every thought, word, and deed.

Scripture Reading: Psalm 15:2, 5b

"He whose walk is blameless and who does what is righteous, who speaks the truth from his heart… He who does these things will never be shaken."

Jehovah-jereh

Dear Lord,

I have experienced this name of yours many times in my lifetime, Jehovah-jereh, Lord Will Provide.

I don't have enough paper to write down all the times and all the ways you have provided for me. I have never truly needed anything that you have not provided.

I'm not really talking about physical needs, Lord, as much as I am emotional and spiritual needs. When I needed to feel loved, you offered your unfailing love. When I was in great fear, you relieved that fear with peace and hope. When I couldn't forgive myself for my past, you showed me 1 John 1:9, "*If we confess our sins, he is faithful and just and will forgive us our sins and purify us from all unrighteousness.*" When I kept bringing up my sins, you showed me the last sentence in Jeremiah 31:34, "*for I will forgive their wickedness and will remember their sins no more.*" I can forget them because you have and you really don't want to talk about them anymore.

You have always been and will always be my Jehovah-jereh.

Shared from the Heart

I think God's name, Jehovah-jereh, can be summed up in the lyrics of this beautiful old hymn, "Great Is Thy Faithfulness" (third verse):

Pardon for sin and a peace that endureth
Thine own dear presence to cheer and to guide
Strength for today and bright hope for tomorrow
Blessings all mine, with ten thousand beside.

Great is they faithfulness
Great is thy faithfulness
All I have needed thy hand hath provided
Great is thy faithfulness, Lord unto me

Scripture Reading: Psalm 108:4

"For great is your love, higher than the heavens; your faithfulness reaches to the skies."

Work or Retire

Dear Lord,

It is a known fact that I am getting older but sometimes I think I'm trying to age too fast for my own good. All I think about is retiring!

When I stop and think about it, I realize and acknowledge that you have given me the ability and the health to work. You have also given me a wonderful job that you and I both know came straight from you. Aging can be a wonderful thing, just like so many other experiences, as long as I do it with your grace and on your timetable. I have a responsibility to do the very best I can and to enjoy my time of labor instead of dreading it.

Lord, please put your joy towards my job back in me and help me to embrace life as it is set before me today.

Shared from the Heart

I was getting older and all I could think about was retiring but God wasn't quite ready for that to happen.

Looking back, there were times when it was hard for me to see my job as a blessing but, believe me, it was.

My job went through a lot of changes over the twenty-one years I was there but God put me there and that was a blessing.

There were seasons of joy and seasons of not so much joy but, through it all, God was there holding me up and carrying me through and HE let me know when it was time to retire.

Scripture Reading: Colossians 3:23-24

"Whatever you do, work at it with all your heart, as working for the Lord, not for men, since you know that you will receive an inheritance from the Lord as a reward."

Temptation

Dear Lord,

Thank you for giving me new insights in familiar stories. I read about the "fall of man" in Genesis 3. What I saw was when we give into temptation, we lose something and we gain something else.

We might lose our innocence and gain shame. We could lose our self-respect and gain self-pity. We stand to lose a lot by giving in to sin and we gain things that we really don't want.

Satan is the "great deceiver." He can certainly help us to see things in a "clouded," unreal manner. He makes sin look good but when we give into it, our eyes are opened and we see it for what it really is: SIN.

Help me, Lord, to live with my eyes wide open and to recognize and stand firm against the trick of the "great deceiver."

Shared from the Heart

We cannot stand up against temptation unless we are prepared. We cannot be prepared if we aren't willing to get into God's Word and memorize, digest, and use it when temptation "comes a-calling." Temptation is not a sin but giving in to it is.

Always be prepared!

Scripture Reading: Ephesians 6:10-17

"Finally, be strong in the Lord and in his mighty power. Put on the full armor of God so that you can take your stand against the devil's schemes. For our struggle is not against flesh and blood, but against the rulers, against the authorities, against the powers of this dark world and against the spiritual forces of evil in the heavenly realms. Therefore put on the full armor of God, so that when the day of evil comes, you may be able to stand your ground, and after you have done everything, to stand. Stand firm then, with the belt of truth buckled around your waist, with the breastplate of righteousness in place and with your feet fitted with the readiness that comes from the gospel of peace. In addition to all this, take up the shield of faith with which you can extinguish all the flaming arrows of the evil one. Take the helmet of salvation and the sword of the Spirit, which is the word of God."

My Hand in Yours

Dear Lord,

Wouldn't it be wonderful to wake up in the morning and feel you tightly holding my hand? Wow! You can't get much more "warm and fuzzy" than that.

If I started every day like that, I should be able to live the day totally "spirit-filled" but that doesn't always happen. Your "spirit" certainly doesn't leave me but I sometimes allow things to push you back—kind of like making you take a "back seat." I'm sorry I do that. I don't really mean to and I certainly know that you are there, no matter if my actions show it or not. I've mentioned this verse in my letters to you many times; I guess it's because it's one of my favorites: "*I will never leave you nor forsake you*" (Hebrews 13:5).

Lord, I completely trust that verse and will always try to act like you are there.

Thank you for holding my hand. I love the feel of it.

Shared from the Heart

Don't you just love the feeling of holding hands with someone you care about? I do. Now, just imagine holding hands with Jesus. Is that cool or what?

That is what he does; he holds our hands no matter what is happening in and around us. We might try to let go of his but he's stronger than we are and his grip is firmer!

Scripture Reading: Galatians 5:25

"Since we live by the Spirit, let us keep in step with the Spirit."

Your Name

Dear Lord,

There's a song that says, "Jesus, Jesus, Jesus, there's just something about that name." What a wonderful name. I love to hear it. When I hear it, I immediately feel a smile in my heart.

Yours is also a strong, powerful name that gives me a feeling of security and causes reverent fear. Like the song says, "Let all heaven and earth proclaim, Jesus, Jesus, Jesus, there's just something about that name."

People everywhere are just living their lives without regard to you at all and that is very sad. Someday, at the sound of your name, everyone everywhere will bow.

Jesus, Jesus, Jesus, I bow before you now.

Shared from the Heart

"Jesus" is a very special name to me and I hate it when I hear his name or the Father's used in irreverent ways.

This may sound a little harsh but sometimes I want to say: "Hey, why don't you use your own name if you want to use profanity and leave my God and Savior out of it?"

Scripture Reading: Philippians 2:9-11

"Therefore God exalted him to the highest place and gave him the name that is above every name, that at the name of Jesus every knee should bow, in heaven and on earth and under the earth, and every tongue confess that Jesus Christ is Lord, to the glory of God the Father."

Drifting or Anchored?

Dear Lord,

Do you ever wonder why I just seem to drift away sometimes? I know you don't have to wonder but I do.

It's not that I'm turning away and living a life of sin but I slowly allow the world to slip in. For example, I stay up too late at night and watch a movie. So what do I do in the morning? Right…I sleep later, which means I have less quiet time with you, or sometimes I don't have time for it at all.

Second example, I'm on a tight budget and I go ahead and buy that sweater that I can't afford and really don't need. What happens then? I can't help someone or some ministry that is really in need and the guilt sets in.

Little by little, I let things take over my time and my thoughts. I start drifting and don't even completely realize it. But, in your infinite mercy, you pull me back and help me to, once again, get "anchored."

Thank you, Lord, for not leaving me out there just drifting through life. You are my anchor.

Shared from the Heart

I love to think of Jesus as my "anchor." I could drift all I wanted but I couldn't go very far because he has me firmly anchored to him.

Because I belong to him, I will never drift totally away or sink into the deep, dark sea of sin. He has me "anchored" to his firm foundation.

Scripture Reading: John 10:10

"I have come that they may have life, and that they may have it more abundantly."

Faith

Dear Lord,

I read this morning a passage from Galatians talking about being justified by faith in you, not the law. What I see is that I am saved by faith alone, not by works or just by following rules and regulations.

There's no way I can do enough to keep myself out of trouble. If I can work myself into heaven, why in the world would you have allowed yourself to be given over to such a horrible death?

You did that for me. I know you did it for all mankind, but I take it very personally—you did it for ME. I don't have to do anything other than put my total trust in you, Almighty God, the one that put this plan into motion before life, as we know it, began. The plan is to bring us back to you, no matter where we are or where we've been. All we need to do is have faith in that plan and the one who is at the center of that plan.

Shared from the Heart

I believe there are people who will not accept Jesus and his plan of salvation because it sounds too easy. They believe you have to do something to earn it. Not so. It's a gift and it's free. The one and only requirement from us is to take that first step and put our faith into the one who loved us enough that he gave up everything. Christ did not die for nothing. He died for us.

Scripture Reading: Galatians 2:19-21

"For through the law I died to the law so that I might live for God. I have been crucified with Christ and I no longer live, but Christ lives in me. The life I live in the body, I live by faith in the Son of God, who loves me and gave himself for me. I do not set aside the grace of God, for if righteousness could be gained through the law, Christ died for nothing."

Memories

Dear Lord,

This time of year, my mind is full of wonderful memories. When I hear the beautiful Christmas carols, I can see my precious mother walking around the house singing "Silent Night." That was her favorite carol and the only one that sticks out in my mind that she ever sang.

You blessed me, Lord, with parents who made sure we knew that Christ was born on Christmas Day. I'm not trying to pretend that my family life was perfect. Even though I went to church without my parents, I was taught about the real "reason for the season" before that saying became popular.

We enjoyed Santa, Rudolph, and Frosty but when it came right down to it, "all was calm and all was bright" because we were taught that our Savior entered the world on this night!

Shared from the Heart

I have great memories of my childhood during Christmas time. As I grow older, there are more and more Christmas memories that include loved ones who are no longer with us.

These memories can be "bitter and sweet." They can hurt because these loved ones aren't here to make new memories with us but they can also touch our hearts, remembering the good times shared around this holiday season.

No matter what our memories are, Jesus needs to be right in the middle of them. After all, it is his birthday!

Scripture Reading: Luke 2:8-11

"And there were shepherds living out in the fields nearby, keeping watch over their flocks at night. An angel of the Lord appeared to them, and the glory of the Lord shone around them, and they were terrified. But the angel said to them, 'Do not be afraid. I bring you good news of great joy that will be for all the people. Today in the town of David, a Savior has been born to you he is Christ the Lord.'"

Emotion or Commitment

Dear Lord,

Sometimes through a special sermon, a beautiful song, or an exciting Bible study, I get all caught up in the emotion of loving and serving you. I want to conquer the world for you and I feel like I could. But life goes on, the emotions die down, and I usually haven't conquered anything.

I think I just learned something. It's not emotions you want or need from me; it's sincere dedication or commitment. With a true, dedicated life, you can accomplish many things.

It's not a one-time dedication; it's getting up every morning and making a commitment that the day is yours and give you full authority. One committed day at a time!

Shared from the Heart

I've got to say that my day turns out a lot more like the Lord intends it to be when I remember to give him complete authority at the start of it.

When I hurry through my quiet time and fail to hand over authority, the day just doesn't seem to run as smoothly as it could. I guess when I'm handing over authority, I'm reminded of my commitment to live a life pleasing to him and him alone.

Scripture Reading: Proverbs 16:3

"Commit to the LORD whatever you do, and your plans will succeed."

"I surrender to You God my Father. Equip me to serve you this day in a well pleasing way."

Love of Money

Dear Lord,

When a person has been blessed with material possessions (money, etc.), what is important is the state of their heart. I can say "thank you" all day long and mean it when I'm saying it but what is my heart holding inside?

Am I wanting to give back to not only you, the giver of all good things (James 1:17), and to others who are in need, or is my heart causing me to be selfish and self-centered?

If I'm not giving to others, why in the world would you give to me? Good question. I happen to believe you have a purpose for the money you allow me to have. I also believe that the condition of my financial portfolio is not as important to you as what I do with what you bless me with. Do I keep it and say "thanks" or do I say thanks by giving it to help others?

I pray, Lord, for a clean heart full of sincere compassion toward others. Please never allow me to love money more than I love you or others.

Shared from the Heart

1 Timothy 6:10 is often quoted as: "Money is the root of all evil." The scripture says: "*For the love of money is a root of all kinds of evil.*"

God's desire is not for us to be without money but when we put money or the accumulation of it first, we have created ourselves an idol... and we know what God thinks about idols!

Scripture Reading: Luke 16:13

"No servant can serve two masters. Either he will hate the one and love the other, or he will be devoted to the one and despise the other. You cannot serve both God and Money."

Willing

Dear Lord,

This morning I was reading in Exodus about the building of the Tabernacle (Tent of Meeting), how you told Moses to have the people who were willing to bring articles to be used for the construction as an offering. You said, several times in this passage, "all who were willing."

What was really amazing was that they gave so much Moses had to tell them to stop; they had already given more than enough.

Wow! Wouldn't it be great if that were a problem today—if all your children found it in their hearts to bring so much to you that there would be more than enough to do all the work to accomplish your purposes? Not just money but everything: their time, their energy, their dedication, and their money or possessions.

That would really be something. I can't speak for all believers, but I can tell you for me this really touched me. I don't want to give to you only out of my abundance but I want to give to you all you deserve—that would be my ALL.

I want to get to the point that you have to say: "STOP, YOU'RE GIVING TOO MUCH!"

Shared from the Heart

There are times that I thought the Israelites had what I call a "wishy-washy" faith. One minute they are high on God and the next minute they are worshipping other gods.

I was nicely surprised when I read this passage in Exodus telling about the Israelites not only giving more than enough but doing it willingly. No one was forcing them to do it; they did it because they wanted to. The result was that there was so much given for this need that they had to stop giving.

Wow! Wouldn't that be nice to see or hear about today?

Scripture Reading: Exodus 36:4-7

"So all the skilled craftsmen who were doing all the work on the sanctuary left their work and said to Moses, 'The people are bringing more than enough for doing the work the LORD commanded to be done.' Then Moses gave an order and they sent this word throughout the camp: 'No man or woman is to make anything else as an offering for the sanctuary.' And so the people were restrained from bringing more, because what they already had was more than enough to do all the work."

Habits/Discipline

Dear Lord,

Do you ever want to say, “Daughter, you’re riding on my last nerve; my patience is running out”? I don’t think you do but I probably should think that so I would make those changes in my life that are so needed.

The two changes I’m thinking about that need to be made or habits changed are:

(1) unhealthy eating habits
(2) no exercise

Both these habits are results of NO DISCIPLINE.

I know at my age it is very important for me to eat right and exercise but I seem to want to ignore that fact. I know I can push these bad habits too far and that’s what has my attention today.

Consequences are coming if I don’t make these changes and make them soon. I know how good it feels when I’m eating right and exercising. I also know it has to make you glad when you see me taking good care of my body, your temple.

All the “self-discipline” in the world will not bring the long-lasting results that I need. I can only do this through your power and your strength and I am asking you for that help.

I am also thanking you right now because I know you are faithful and will help me and see me through with this little “discipline” problem.

Shared from the Heart

I have a bad habit of trying to do things or make changes using my own will power. That power is no power at all because I'm not trusting and relying on my real power: Jesus.

I cannot tell you how many diets I've been on or how many exercise programs I've tried unsuccessfully. It's not the diets or exercise programs that failed; it was me.

The reason these programs failed was my reliance on myself to stick to them and not turning it over to Jesus. Yes, I have to use self-discipline but I need to get this self-discipline by counting on Jesus to strengthen, guide, and direct my every move.

Scripture Reading: Psalm 28:7

"The LORD is my strength and my shield; my heart trusts in him and I am helped. My heart leaps for joy and I will give thanks to him in song."

Thank you LORD for this message today. You are my strength and my shield.
June 17, 2017

Breath of God

Dear Lord,

Yesterday was an amazing day. When you literally stopped that truck behind me from crashing into me, I was at a loss for words (momentarily). I even closed my eyes and waited for the crash but you stepped between me and what could have been a terrible accident.

Of all the times in my life that you have taken care of me, and there have been many, this one felt different. I can't remember a time when I felt your presence like I did at that moment. It was so real that I felt your breath upon me.

I know that accidents happen but for some reason you did not allow it yesterday. It wasn't good driving on my part or the other driver's; it was you and you alone.

Sometimes I try to look hard at an experience to see what I could learn from it. Sometimes I see something and sometimes I don't. What I learned from yesterday's experience was that life can rock along, everything as usual, and suddenly change comes without a warning. No matter what happens, you are there with your presence, your peace, and comfort like no one else can be.

You surrounded me with your wings and for that I say, "Thank you."

Shared from the Heart

Most of the time when I really feel God's amazing presence it is during low times or scary moments. When you're going through dark times, there is absolutely nothing better than feeling God's holy presence surrounding you.

We can either ignore his presence or we can bask in it and allow it to carry us through whatever the circumstance may be.

Scripture Reading: Psalm 91:1-6

"He who dwells in the shelter of the Most High will rest in the shadow of the Almighty. I will say of the LORD, He is my refuge and my fortress, my God in whom I trust. Surely he will save you from the fowler's snare and from the deadly pestilence. He will cover you with his feathers and under his wings you will find refuge; his faithfulness will be your shield and rampart. You will not fear the terror of night nor the arrow that flies by day, not the pestilence that stalks in the darkness nor the plague that destroys at midday."

Belonging

Dear Lord,

Okay, I love music and how you use it. I listened to another song that I've heard a million times but one little phrase jumped out at me today. That phrase was: "I belong to Jesus." I've probably sung those words or something like them a million times before but today "I belong to Jesus" made by heart soar.

It's common knowledge in the life of a believer that you purchased us through the sacrifice of your life, through your blood spilled out for everyone on the cross. Somehow just saying the words "I belong to Jesus" gives me hope and security and a worth that I've never really thought that much about before.

I have a wonderful family that I "belong" to but first and foremost I "belong" to you. I love that! I'm not just someone down here living; I'm someone you know and someone you consider one of yours.

I wouldn't want to belong to anyone else!

Shared from the Heart

There's a lot of stuff that goes on in this world around us that can make us feel lost, lonely, and out of sorts. The one thing that keeps me going is the fact that "I belong to Jesus." That statement by itself can snap me out of my "poor-me" state faster than you can say, "Heaven is my home."

Scripture Reading: John 1:12-13

"Yet to all who received him, to those who believed in his name, he gave the right to become children of God—children born not of natural descent, nor of human decision or a husband's will, but born of God."

Rejoice

Dear Lord,

Worry, where does it get you? Being anxious, how does it help? All these two things get me is stressed, confused, and probably a little depressed.

Your Word teaches me to "rejoice in the Lord always." I'm not taking this to mean to rejoice in your hardships but to rejoice through your hardships.

Rejoice that I have a relationship with you, "the lover of my soul," the one true and faithful God. Rejoice because whatever is happening, I'm not alone. You are always with me. You are there with that wonderful peace of yours that goes beyond human understanding.

I'm talking about the kind of peace that I haven't just read about but that I've felt and cherished many, many times. The kind of peace that only you can give. The kind of peace that you don't hold back but that you generously give when asked for and sometimes even before it's asked for.

Now there's something to rejoice about!

Shared from the Heart

Rejoicing through your hardships is probably not the easiest thing to do but it can be done. During a hard time, try to remember who you belong to and how much you are loved.

Rejoice in the fact that God never promises us anything he doesn't follow through with. He said he would never leave us and we can totally believe it.

Rejoice in the fact that when this life as we know it is done, we will see our Savior face to face and have all of eternity to rejoice.

Scripture Reading: Philippians 4:4-7

"Rejoice in the Lord always. I will say it again: Rejoice. Let your gentleness be evident to all. The Lord is near. Do not be anxious about anything but in everything by prayer and petition, with thanksgiving, present your requests to God. And the peace of God which transcends all understanding, will guard your hearts and your minds in Christ Jesus."

Acquittal

Dear Lord,

You know, there are times that Satan is at his old tricks. Yes, his very old tricks. He tries to bring up my past transgressions and he's working toward that "let's make her feel guilty and unworthy—that'll make her useless for a while" feeling.

I guess he forgot that when I went to you for forgiveness of all my sins, I was acquitted. I was tried and acquitted and cannot be tried again. If I were tried again, that would be "double jeopardy."

So, when Satan comes at me, and he will, I can stand firm in the fact that I don't carry those sins anymore. You have given me complete forgiveness. I have been set free for now and all eternity.

Shared from the Heart

I doubt that I'm the only person who has received the Lord's forgiveness for something but finds themselves talking about that same sin to him again. Not only talking about it but I keep bringing it up even when I feel his Spirit telling me to "let it go."

If God can forgive and forget, why is it so hard for us to do? I believe that Satan loves to remind us of our past sins and failures to make us feel useless and unworthy. He knows what buttons to push and he loves pushing them.

There's one thing for us to remember when this happens: we have the power and the strength of the Holy Spirit living in us, which means Satan doesn't stand a chance!

Scripture Reading: John 8:36

"If the Son sets you free, you are free indeed."

Pride

Dear Lord,

One of the things I have learned over the years is that there is one sin that seems to trip me up the most and that is pride.

Pride has been the cause of many downfalls in my life. Now, pride is not always a bad thing but "self-absorbing" pride is.

In order to be the person you desire for me to be and to have the life you desire for me, the one thing I have to do is lay down the most difficult trait I possess: self-absorbing pride.

To make this change, I have to turn over control and allow you to work in and through me. Turning over control has to be a daily act of my will.

When you are in control, my pride has been put in its proper place.

Shared from the Heart

If we are walking in God's will, there really isn't a lot of room for self-absorbing pride. God wants us to put him first in all things and if we are doing that, pride shouldn't be an issue.

Self-absorbing pride should have no home in a believer's heart.

Scripture Reading: Proverbs 16:18-10

"Pride goes before destruction, a haughty spirit before a fall. Better to be lowly in spirit and among the oppressed than to share plunder with the proud. Whoever gives heed to instruction prospers, and blessed is he who trusts in the LORD."

Jehovah-Sabaoth

Dear Lord,

You are definitely Jehovah-Sabaoth, Lord of Host/Lord Almighty, to me today.

With age sometimes comes worry. I catch myself getting anxious all of a sudden about car accidents or major health issues that could cause me to lose someone I love. I was beginning to get obsessed with these thoughts when I read your name, Jehovah-Sabaoth, Lord of Host/ Lord Almighty. I Samuel 1:3-11

You are God, the Lord Almighty. Nothing happens to me or my family that is not known by you. I believe that you are prepared and capable to get me or anyone else through whatever happens in life.

I don't want to experience any of these tragic circumstances but I acknowledge that they could happen and I place my trust in your character.

You promise to be with me through anything—good, bad, and ugly—and you've never broken a promise to me yet.

You always have been and always will be Jehovah-Sabaoth, the Lord of Host/Lord Almighty.

Shared from the Heart

Do we really think we can change things with worry? I've never been a "big" worrier but as I've grown older, worry has become a little more active in my life.

I allow myself to think about a lot of "what ifs" that can really play havoc with your inner peace.

If we live long enough, we will experience hard times and, yes, tragedies. We cannot avoid these things but we can trust in the one true God that will never leave us, just like he promised, no matter what's happening.

Scripture Reading: Psalms 100:3-4

"Know that the LORD is God. It is he who made us and we are his; we are his people, the sheep of his pasture. Enter his gates with thanksgiving and his courts with praise; give thanks to him and praise his name."

Miracles

Dear Lord,

In the Bible, people followed you immediately after they saw the miracles you performed—miracles like healing the blind so they could see (John 9:25), healing the paralyzed so they could walk (Mark 2:11), raising the dead (John 11:43), and feeding five thousand people with two fish and five loaves of bread (Matthew 14:17).

What kind of miracles are happening around me every day that I'm missing?

- The miracle of a life turned around by your grace and forgiveness (which proves you listen to prayers)
- The miracle of a life hanging on when medical logic says their body should have already given up
- The miracle of your wonderful provision day after day
- The miracle of your written Word sustained over thousands of years without error and proving every day that you are who you say you are.

Lord, you perform miracles every day. Help me not to overlook them and to always give you praise for them.

Shared from the Heart

God is still in the miracle business today. You hear of wonderful miracles like a child needing heart surgery because his heart is on the wrong side of his body but when last-minute testing is done, lo and behold, everything is in its proper place. A precious miracle!

I also believe that God performs not only big miracles like that one but also loves performing little miracles every day. We just have to be looking a little closer to see them but they are there!

Scripture Reading: Psalms 103:2-5

"Praise the LORD, O my soul, and forget not all his benefits—who forgives all your sins and heals all your diseases, who redeems your life from the pit and crowns you with love and compassion, who satisfies your desires with good things so that your youth is renewed like the eagle's."

Jehovah-nissi

Dear Lord,

Your name today is Jehovah-nissi, Lord Is My Banner.

When I go to home and garden shows or other exhibitions, I see banners all over the place telling people whom that particular booth belongs to. The banner declares ownership. What kind of banner do I wear? Who owns me?

I know who owns me but does everyone I come in contact with know? I want my banner to be so obvious that there is no doubt. I want people to say of me, "There's no doubt about it—she belongs to Jesus."

When I lift my hands toward heaven, I want it to mean something. I want it to relay a message that says, "She totally relies and trusts in the one that bears the name Jehovah-nissi, Lord Is My Banner."

Shared from the Heart

There was a time period in my past that I'm not proud of, but it's there nonetheless. During this time, someone I knew was shocked when they found out I was a Christian. I will never forget as long as I live the look on their face and the pain in my heart. I vowed right then that people would know who I really belonged to by my words and, more importantly, by my actions.

Scripture Reading: Exodus 17:12-16a

When Moses' hands grew tired, they took a stone and put it under him and he sat on it. Aaron and Hur held his hands up—one on one side, one on the other—so that his hands remained steady till sunset. So Joshua overcame the Amalekite army with the sword. Then the LORD said to Moses, 'Write this on a scroll as something to be remembered and make sure that Joshua hears it, because I will completely blot out the memory of Amalek from under heaven.' Moses built an altar and called it The LORD is my Banner. He said, 'For hands were lifted up to the throne of the LORD.'"

Decorating Dilemma

Dear Lord,

Just between you and me, I'm wrestling with a little decision that I need your help with. I need your help because I know you care about all the things in my life—big and small.

The dilemma is: do I take down your picture that I have had on my wall forever or do I leave it up?

If I take your picture down, will you be upset? Why am I taking it down? I'm not sure. If I'm taking it down for decorating sense, is that wrong or right? Are you offended or do you find humor in my plight?

When I look at it logically, I know we really don't know what you looked like. This is just a composite of what someone thinks that you probably looked like. Just because I take you off my wall doesn't mean I've taken you out of my life.

On the other hand, when people walk in my home, they know to whom I belong. But, then again, just because I've got a picture of you on my wall doesn't mean I truly belong to you. My life, my commitment, and declaration of my dependence on you says I belong to you, not the decoration on my wall.

Okay, I think the picture is coming down. You are still the center of my life even if you are not hanging in the center of my living room wall.

But, then again, I really like looking at your picture! Oh, what to do!!

Shared from the Heart

I choose to believe that God has a great sense of humor. He has to so he can handle us with all the grace that he does. I also believe that God is delighted in the fact that we talk to him about the smaller, insignificant things that pass through our lives. He cares about everything that affects us, both big and small.

In case you are interested, the picture is still on my wall!

Scripture Reading: James 1:5

"If any of you lacks wisdom, he should ask God, who gives generously to all without finding fault, and it will be given to him."

End Times

Dear Lord,

This world has gotten crazy. I have no idea, Lord, when your return will be but I do feel we have entered into the "end times."

If this is true, what should I be busy doing? There is an easy answer. I should be staying alert and taking every opportunity to show and tell the "good news" to those I know and don't know, related or not. What is the "good news"? I believe John 3:16 says it all.

I'm asking for your wisdom, strength, and boldness to be your faithful messenger. I really don't want to miss someone in heaven because I failed to be the light and the salt (Matthew 5:13-14) that you tell us to be.

Lord, let my light shine and my mouth speak with boldness the "good news" that you are the only answer to this crazy world. This world will someday no longer exist but you will be forever, just as we that trust in you will be forever.

Praise you, God!

Shared from the Heart

This world is so out of control it's hard for me not to believe that we could be in the end times. Of course, no one but God truly knows but he has given us signs. These signs should have all believers working harder than ever in spreading the gospel of Jesus Christ.

God doesn't want anyone to miss out on spending eternity with him and he wants to use us to see that all people know that truth.

Scripture Reading: John 3:16-18

"For God so loved the world that he gave his one and only son, that whoever believes in him shall not perish but have everlasting life. For God did not send his son into the world to condemn the world, but to save the world through him. Whoever believes in him is not condemned, but whoever does not believe stands condemned already because he has not believed in the name of God's one and only son."

The Cross

Dear Lord,

Here I am on another beautiful Easter morning, standing in awe of you.

This morning, I heard a song that had a line in it that said something like this: "Why did they have to nail his hands when his love would have held him there?" Wow!

All through your Word, I read about your love, from cover to cover, but today something really hit me. There is nothing that would have deterred you from sacrificing yourself for me. The love you had for mankind was stronger than any nail or anything else that might try to hold you back.

You were completely determined to make a way for me to spend eternity with you. That was your goal—eternity with mankind, and you had me in mind. That is so mind-boggling.

Your plan didn't stop at the cross. You were victorious over death and so will I be.

Shared from the Heart

I just recently lost someone very special in my life. Even though she lived a good life and died at ninety-nine years of age, you are never really ready to let a loved one go.

The one bright star in this loss is that I know she's not in the grave. She loved Jesus and because of what he accomplished on the cross, she, too, is saying: "Death has been swallowed up in victory."

Scripture Reading: 1 Corinthians 15:54-57

"When the perishable has been clothed with the imperishable, and the mortal with immortality, then the saying that is written will come true: 'Death has been swallowed up in victory.' The sting of death is sin, and the power of sin is the law. But thanks be to God, he gives us the victory through our Lord, Jesus Christ."

Where Are the Tears?

Dear Lord,

As you know, I just went through one of the most difficult times of my life. Waiting for a loved one to take their last breath will rip your heart out.

There were times that I was so tired and scared, I couldn't even cry. I felt the tears inside but very few fell on the outside, so where were they? It's not always the best thing not to cry. Sometimes it needs to come out.

When you said in Hebrews 13:5: "*I will never leave you or forsake you,*" you weren't kidding. As I paced the halls at the nursing home, you were there. As I stood over her bedside, you were there. As I laid my weary head down at night, you were there.

When I finally let all those tears out, you refreshed my soul. As always, you were there.

Shared from the Heart

I honestly don't know how people who do not claim Jesus as their Savior can survive the really difficult times that we all have to face.

I have had to rely on his presence and his comfort many times over the years and I have to say if I did not have him to hang on to, I'm not sure I would have made it. He at times had to be my very breath.

Scripture Reading: Jeremiah 31:25

"I will refresh the weary and satisfy the faint."

Giants

Dear Lord,

I think I just met another giant! When your workplace starts downsizing and you are in the line of fire, that is a giant.

You know why I'm not freaking out, Lord? It has to be because defeating giants is one of your specialties. You didn't do it only once back in David's time (1Samuel 17), but you have helped me through many giants in my lifetime alone.

Well, here we are again, facing another one. This time my age is a factor. Early retirement (really not that early) is not my choice but it could be the company's choice.

This downsizing thing took me by surprise but it certainly didn't surprise you. There's a song that just came to my mind, "Maker of the Road." There's a line that says, "I don't have to worry, because you have gone before me, Maker of the Road."

I don't need to be fearful because you've never let me down before and you won't start now. We have a history, you and I, and I feel comfort and strength in that! You and I will be conquerors—one giant at a time!

Shared from the Heart

What are the giants in our lives that can take us captive? It could be the loss of a loved one, loss of a job, loss of a relationship, financial problems, or health issues.

There are two things to remember: (1) God is not surprised at what is happening, and (2) he is big enough and strong enough to carry us through to the other side. Nothing is too big for him.

Scripture Reading: Psalm 18:29

"With your help I can advance against a troop; with my God, I can scale a wall."

The Flood

Dear Lord,

I'm thinking a terminally ill sister, a shaky job situation, finances, and an aging body should be enough for one person at one time. Evidently, three house floodings in a month were needed for extra measure.

The first time the house flooded, I panicked. The second time, it was almost a non-event, just a big pain. The third time, depression set in. I believe my cry was, "I don't know how much more I can handle."

The problem with that statement is "me" handling it. I can't, at least not with my own power. In Isaiah 40:29, it says, "*He gives strength to the weary and increases the power of the weak.*" Well, Lord, I am feeling weary and weak but I have a feeling strength is on the way!

One thing I've learned during this time is that there is no flood too deep for you. I can't walk on water but I don't have to; I'm being carried.

Shared from the Heart

Have you ever thought in your head, "God, enough is enough. I cannot handle one more thing"? I have. God does know our limits. He may push those limits (humanly speaking) but I truly believe he won't push beyond what we can take.

Do I understand why so many things can happen to one person in a short period of time? No, but I do believe that the Lord is our helper, our rock, our provider, our shield, our protector, and, yes, our strength.

Scripture Reading: Hebrews 13:6

"We say with confidence, the Lord is my helper; I will not be afraid. What can man do to me?"

Repayment

Dear Lord,

There are times when I do things for others that need to be just between you and me. I respect that and I try to be obedient. I would much rather have my reward in heaven than here on earth, where it's temporal and not eternal.

But, Lord, when you, in your own perfect timing, turn around and reward the giver with the exact amount that was given, that's almost too much to keep quiet about. It would be hard not to tell everyone so they can see how real, how loving, and how kind you are and that you don't ignore your children when they obey your "holy nudging."

I know it's important, when we are blessed, to use that blessing to help others. When I bless others, Proverbs 19:17 comes to life: "*He who is kind to the poor lends to the LORD, and He will reward him for what he has done.*"

I always want to be a giver because of what you've given to me. I have never not had my own needs met, not once, because you are faithful.

Proverbs 11:25 says: "*A generous man will prosper; he who refreshes others will himself be refreshed.*" Amen and amen.

Shared from the Heart

I want to be a giver because God is a giver. I don't ever want to give expecting God to "return the favor" but only because my heart tells me it's the right thing to do.

Giving to someone when the only other person who knows about it is God is the most wonderful feeling in the world. So, why don't we do it more often?

Scripture Reading: Matthew 6:1-4

"Be careful not to do your acts of righteousness before men, to be seen by them. If you do, you will have no reward from your Father in heaven. So when you give to the needy, do not announce it with trumpets, as the hypocrites do in the synagogues and on the streets, to be honored by men. I tell you the truth, they have received their reward in full. But when you give to the needy, do not let your left hand know what your right hand is doing, so that your giving may be in secret. Then your Father, who sees what is done in secret, will reward you."

Real Love

Dear Lord,

I watched a movie titled "Passion of the Christ" and was overwhelmed with sadness. Not sadness as in "Oh, Jesus, I'm sorry they did that to you" but the kind of sadness that gets your attention and makes you look deep down into your soul. Sadness that makes me realize that I don't always treat you the way you deserve.

You tell me in your Word, "*Love the Lord with all your heart and with all your soul and with all your mind and with all your strength*" (Mark 12:30). I believe that's how you love me.

There's a song that says, "You took the fall and thought of me above all." You let them nail you to a cross just to give me the opportunity to spend eternity in heaven with you and then there are times I have to make myself read my Bible? What kind of love and devotion is that? You gave up everything for me and all you ask in return is my love.

Lord, please let the vision of your tortured body always be a reminder of what real love is—sacrificial and unconditional.

Shared from the Heart

As long as I live, I do not believe I will ever fully understand God's complete, unconditional love for me. Just because I don't understand it doesn't change the fact that it's real. My human mind might not be able to compute the depth of his love but it's there all the same and I can feel it all around me.

Don't you wish we were all capable of loving God the way he loves us?

Scripture Reading: Colossians 1:19-20

"For God was pleased to have all his fullness dwell in him, and through him to reconcile to himself all things, whether things on earth or things in heaven, by making peace through his blood, shed on the cross."

Let Go!

Dear Lord,

I like to take scripture personally. When I read Matthew 18:22-35, the "Parable of the Unmerciful Servant," I felt you talking to me. You simply told me that you had forgiven me for all my past, present, and future debts; now I have to do the same with others. You also said that when someone tells me they are sorry, to let you be the judge of their sincerity.

Your instructions to me are to keep my own heart and mind clean before you. Stop dragging up old offenses and don't be a part of keeping them alive.

When I say, "I forgive," I have to mean it and I have to LET IT GO!

Shared from the Heart

Forgiveness is a must, not an option. When we fail to forgive, we are hurting ourselves more than the other person. The weight of holding back forgiveness is heavy and burdensome. If we are holding on to unforgiveness, we've got to get rid of it!

Scripture Reading: Matthew 18:22

"Jesus answered, I tell you, not seven times but seventy-seven times."

Intercessor

Dear Lord,

I was reading Hebrews chapter 7, verse 25, and it says, "*Therefore, He is able to save completely those who come to God through Him because He always lives to intercede for them.*"

When I think about that verse, the word "completely" stands out. The study portion of my Bible says, "No one can add to what Jesus did to save us; our past, present and future sins are forgiven, and Jesus is with the Father as a sign that our sins our forgiven." To me, this "complete" means it's done—nothing else is necessary; you've given me the complete package. My sins are not only forgiven but you are my intercessor with the Father.

You, Jesus, are my very own private priest. I should live daily in the confidence of that statement. Fear of any kind should never be part of who I am. What security this verse contains. You, Lord, intercede for me. Now that truly warms my soul!

Another word that stuck out was "always," which means I will never be without an intercessor, someone on my side.

Completely and always—it can't get any better than that!

Shared from the Heart

Don't you just love it when you know for sure that someone is on your side—that someone has your back?

Just bask in the fact that this someone can be Jesus. He even discusses us with the Father. How awesome is that!

Scripture Reading: Hebrews 7:23-26

"Now there have been many of those priests, since death prevented them from continuing in office, but because Jesus lives forever, he has a permanent priesthood. Therefore, he is able to save completely those who come to God through him because he always lives to intercede for them. Such a high priest meets our need—one who is holy, blameless, pure, set apart from sinners, exalted above the heavens."

Persevere

Dear Lord,

Sometimes sticking with something you have called me to do seems really hard when I think it's time for it to be done. Then I remember it's not my place to call something "done"; it's the God of my heart that calls something finished. I have to see it through to the very end.

To persevere, I must cover the task with prayer and with action. I can't give up because it looks hopeless or it feels like it's way over my head. Nothing you truly start is hopeless and you will equip me for whatever you call me to do.

Help me, Lord, to be strong in you and keep my mind positive and not dwell on the negative.

Shared from the Heart

I cannot tell you how patient God has been with me. I have been writing these letters to him for over ten years and I'm just now getting them wrapped up.

I do believe that when God calls us to do something, he will bring it to fruition. I'm really glad that just because of my procrastination he didn't decide to use someone else for this assignment. He started it and he will finish it, with or without me. I'm glad it was with me.

Scripture Reading: Galatians 6:9

"Let us not become weary in doing good, for at the proper time we will reap a harvest if we do not give up."

Jehovah—Self-Existent One

Dear Lord,

Your name today is Jehovah, Self-Existent One. I could ask the question, "Where did you come from?" but the fact that everything started with you brings comfort to me. No one created you, no one made you—you just were! "*In the beginning God created the heavens and the earth" (Genesis 1:1).*

This gives me complete security in trusting you with my life and my eternity. I'm not trusting and depending on someone who could have been created with faults; I'm trusting in Jehovah, the one that began it all. I love that!

This world didn't just happen and humans didn't just evolve. You and your love brought everything into existence. You did this for a reason and you did it with a plan in mind.

Your reason was to spend "forever" with me and your plan included coming to earth in the human form of Jesus and dying on a cruel cross. Your plan didn't stop there. You rose from the grave and ascended back to heaven. Humans could never come up with a plan like that or accomplish such a plan. But you, Jehovah, the Self-Existent One, knew what you were going to do from the beginning and accomplished everything you set out to do.

Thank you, Lord!

Shared from the Heart

I cannot tell you how sad it makes me when I read about someone who places their faith in science. Science!

How can science love you when no one else seems to? How can science comfort you when your heart is broken? How does science guide you when you've lost your way and strengthen you when you are weak? How can science promise and provide eternal hope? It can't.

Scripture Reading: John 1:1-4, 14

"In the beginning was the Word and the Word was with God and the Word was God. He was with God in the beginning. Through him all things were made; without him nothing was made that has been made. In him was life, and that life was the light of men."

"The Word became flesh and made his dwelling among us. We have seen his glory, the glory of the One and Only who came from the Father, full of grace and truth."

In Your Arms

Dear Lord,

I was reading "Our Daily Bread" this morning and couldn't believe what I was reading. You always supply my every need, especially in times of sorrow.

There is a quote in the devotion section from author Susan Lenskes that says, "It's all right—questions, pain and stabbing anger can be poured out to the Infinite One and He will not be damaged… For we beat on His chest from within the Circle of His arms."

Wow! That gives me goose bumps just thinking about it. After a long battle, my precious sister is now with you and I'm in the circle of your arms telling you how much I'm going to miss her and, yes, I have many questions. "Why did she have to suffer so long?" and "Why did she go at what I consider too young an age?" would be a couple of questions.

I am sad but not for her. I'm sad for me and the rest of the family. She is gone but you are not. I have to tell you, Lord, I love the comfort of the "circle of your arms."

Shared from the Heart

I love hugs and I'm not ashamed of it. Just imagine when everything in you is hurting, like your insides are being ripped out, and being wrapped up in the big arms of God. There he is, patting your back and promising you that you will get through this and promising to stay right there with you through it all.

There is no better place to be when life is trying to tear you apart than in the circle of the great I AM's arms.

Scripture Reading: Psalm 55:6-8

"I said, oh, that I had the wings of a dove! I would fly away and be at rest. I would fly far away and stay in the desert; I would hurry to my place of shelter, far from the tempest and storm."

Love of Plastic

Dear Lord,

What happens when we let buying things on credit get out of control? Our debt becomes unmanageable and we worry about it all the time. We pull out those plastic cards, use them again and again, and then start worrying about using them. It's a ridiculous cycle.

In Peter, you tell me that I must cast my anxiety upon you, even if I've caused that anxiety myself. If I don't give it to you, it will consume me. When I allow that to happen, Satan wins!

When I'm consumed with my "self-made" debt, I'm not praying for the lost and hurting like I should; I'm not finding ways to encourage others and I'm not worshipping you with my whole heart—all because of stupid plastic cards and my desire to have more stuff!

There's nothing wrong with "stuff" as long as it doesn't become so important that it becomes an idol. When I let it consume me, it's an idol.

Only you can relieve my anxiety and only you can give me the ability to overcome. I put my heart and my hand in yours. I again trust you completely.

Shared from the Heart

I would love to blame Satan on all my bad spending decisions but most of the blame needs to be pointed at me. I'm the one who once loved to take those stupid plastic cards out and use them even when I felt a holy nudging not to. I was the one making the decision to keep spending when I knew it was getting out of control.

Credit cards do not have to be a bad thing as long as we allow God to be in control, not us, and never ignore a "holy nudging."

Scripture Reading: 1 Peter 5:6-9

"Humble yourselves, therefore, under God's mighty hand, that he may lift you up in due time. Cast all your anxiety on him because he cares for you. Be self-controlled and alert. Your enemy the devil prowls around like a roaring lion looking for someone to devour. Resist him, standing firm in the faith, because you know that your brothers throughout the world are undergoing the same kind of sufferings."

Drink Offering

Dear Lord,

What does "*being poured out as a drink offering*" (2 Timothy 4:6) mean? It should mean to allow you to use me in any way you so choose. If that includes losing my life for your sake, then so be it.

More than likely I won't have to lose my life for the sake of the gospel, like Paul did, but the question is, "Am I willing to?" Of course, I want to say yes but I don't think I can know the answer to that for sure until it happens.

What I can do in the here and now is to live for you and put you in the proper place in my life. The proper place would be the "throne of my heart." If I allow that, everything that happens will be your will and I will be able to be obedient, even if it means my very life.

Hand's

Isa. 55-12
65-2
1-15 *
30:21
41:10

9-972-874-9643

Ps. 121:5
138:7
139:10 lead me & Thy right hand
Shall hold me

Prov: 4:27
12:15
24:26

Luke 20:42

Eccl. 10:2

Saturday March 24, 2018

orning Meds. → 8:00 A.M. – Lina A

ntibiotics → " " 4-15 *

Evening Meds. → 5:05 P.M. – Extra

so Antibiotics → " "

owellMoro) Small → " " P.M.

XANAX → 7:00 P.M. – EU

Shared from the Heart

Living in the will of God is a safe place to be but it is also a scary place. We know God is always with us but we also know that he may require from us things that we are not sure we are able to do or maybe even want to do.

There is one thing we can rely on and that is whatever we find ourselves called to do, we will be equipped with the wisdom, ability, strength, and grace to see it through.

Scripture Reading: 2 Timothy 4:6-8

"For I am already being poured out like a drink offering, and the time has come for my departure. I have fought the good fight, I have finished the race, I have kept the faith. Now there is in store for me the crown of righteousness, which the Lord, the righteous Judge, will award to me on that day—and not only to me, but also to all who have longed for his appearing."

A Light

Dear Lord,

I'm amazed when I think about how long you have preserved your Word. When your Word was written, there were no typewriters, computers, discs, or even paper as we know it today. But, still, I am holding in my hand your very Word. That can only be an act of the one true God, you.

In your Word, you left me many instructions and one of them tells me to be a light in the world (Matthew 5:14). There have been times when I was not always a very bright light but I will not despair because you also tell me about your mercies that are new every morning (Lamentations 3:23-24). Because of your great mercy, I have a chance every morning to wake up and be that bright light.

Praise you, God, that you give me the chance and ability to be your light in this darkened world.

Shared from the Heart

I'm not proud of the fact that my light has not always shone as bright as it should have.

I am proud of the fact that, each new day God chooses to allow me to live, I am going to take the opportunity as he places it before me and share his light with people in this crazy world of ours who so desperately need to see "the Light."

Scripture Reading: Matthew 5:14-16

"You are the light of the world. A city on a hill cannot be hidden. Neither do people light a lamp and put it under a bowl. Instead they put it on its stand, and it gives light to everyone in the house. In the same way, let your light shine before men, that they may see your good deeds and praise your Father in heaven."

Your Enemies

Dear Lord,

It's easy to love those who love you but it's really not so easy to love those who really don't like you or you feel have wronged you in some way.

Your Word is very clear that I must "love my enemies." I don't know if I have any real enemies but there are people who don't really care for me. To be a good witness and a godly one, it doesn't matter how someone feels about me; it only matters how I treat them.

I was raised on the scripture: "*Do unto others as you would have them do unto you*" (Luke 6:31). If this verse were taken more seriously and people lived this verse, we would have a lot fewer divorces, less child abuse, fewer murders, and all that other rotten stuff!

I think, Lord, that if I try to make it a habit to repeat this verse several times a day in my head and let it become the basis for all my thoughts and my actions, then I can make a difference in my small world as I know it.

Shared from the Heart

Don't you wish everyone everywhere would live by the motto: "Treat others as you want to be treated"? Logic tells me that is not going to happen in our world as we know it today.

Treating our enemies (strong word) with kindness, gentleness, and goodness is sometimes hard but it is the right thing to do.

Scripture Reading: Luke 6:27-31

"But I tell you who hear me: love your enemies, do good to those who hate you, bless those who curse you, pray for those who mistreat you. If someone strikes you on one cheek, turn to him the other also. If someone takes your cloak, do not stop him from taking your tunic. Give to everyone who asks you, and if anyone takes what belongs to you, do not demand it back. Do to others as you would have them do to you."

Depress and Lift

Dear Lord,

Wow! Reading these scriptures in Romans can depress you and lift you up all at the same time. They are a little depressing because they show me who I really am and what's inside me at birth. But then, thanks to you, Lord, I can see the light at the end of the tunnel. That light is you, "the light of the world" (Matthew 5:14).

Yes, without you, I am hopeless and defeated but with you, I have hope eternal.

I will keep doing things I really don't want to do but I will ask, just as Paul did, who would rescue me and my answer would be the same as his: Jesus Christ, our only Savior.

I don't have to be depressed because you have lifted me up.

Shared from the Heart

I really get upset with myself when I keep doing the same thing over and over. Each time I wonder how I got back to the same place as I was before. It takes a little pressure off knowing that great men of the Bible, like Apostle Paul, struggled with the same issue.

The good news is that no matter how many times we fail, God is there to lift us up, time after time after time.

Scripture Reading: Romans 7:15-25a

"I do not understand what I do. For what I want to do I do not do, but what I hate I do. And if I do what I do not want to do, I agree that the law is good. As it is, it is no longer I myself who do it, but it is sin living in me. I know that nothing good lives in me that is, in my sinful nature. For I have the desire to do what is good, but I cannot carry it out. For what I do is not the good I want to do; no, the evil I do not want to do—this I keep on doing. Now if I do what I do not want to do, it is no longer I who do it, but it is sin living in me that does it. So I find this law at work: When I want to do good, evil is right there with me. For in my inner being I delight in God's law; but I see another law at work in the members of my body, waging war against the law of my mind and making me a prisoner of the law of sin at work within my members. What a wretched man I am! Who will rescue me from this body of death? Thanks be to God—through Jesus Christ our Lord."

Worship

Dear Lord,

Our pastor recently gave us the meaning of the word "worship" that is used in the story in Matthew when the three wise men came to worship you. The meaning is "to kiss towards, intensely adore."

I love that! Every time I bow my head, raise my hands, or get on my knees, I want to keep that meaning running through my mind and filling my heart and spirit: "kiss towards, intensely adore."

"Intensely adore" is definitely the perfect meaning. I don't want that definition to fill me just when I'm in church. I want that to be my way of life. I want that to be the result of everything I do. Let everything I do reflect that I "intensely adore" you, my Savior, my King forever.

Shared from the Heart

I love and adore Jesus but what do my attitude and actions say to the outside world? Do they truly reflect love and adoration or are they telling a completely different story?

Scripture Reading: Matthew 2:10-11

"When they saw the star, they were overjoyed. On coming to the house, they saw the child with his mother, Mary, and they bowed down and worshiped him."

Afraid to Speak

Dear Lord,

Why am I afraid to say something to people I love about your love and their relationship with you? Yes, they may get upset with me and feel I'm acting like Miss Righteous but what is the worst thing that could happen? They could get mad, upset, and don't talk to me for a while. What's the best thing that could happen? Their relationship with you could be restored and if they don't have a relationship with you, their eternal destination could change.

It's my responsibility and my honor to speak of you openly and humbly to all people, especially to family. I should not do this just because I love them but because I love you!

All I have to do is speak in the spirit of love and kindness and let you do the rest.

Shared from the Heart

It can be quite risky to witness to a family member because they usually know all your good and bad points and sometimes don't mind pointing them out. But it's worth the risk if, by your witness, they come to know Jesus or their separated relationship with Jesus is restored.

When God asks you to talk to someone about him, we must do it but we also must do it in a loving, kind, and humble manner. Remember, we're just the witness; he does all the work and deserves all the glory.

Scripture Reading: Ephesians 4:2

"Be completely humble and gentle, be patient, bearing with one another in love."

Elevator Ride

Dear Lord,

I was going through an old journal this morning and on one sheet all by itself I had written, "Only place we can get on God's spiritual elevator is in the basement of our lives."

Now, where in the world that came from I have no earthly idea. I'm pretty sure I didn't come up with it nor does it even sound vaguely familiar but it is a very profound statement.

I'm assuming since I wrote it down in my book it meant something to me at the time. Was my spiritual life in the basement and I needed uplifting? Did something happen that brought me low in my spirit?

I know when everything around me is falling apart, I'm more willing and receptive to opening up to you and allowing you to minister to me and heal whatever is hurting at the time. I believe that this statement probably reminded me that in those "down" times, when I'm completely broken and at my lowest point, you are there, ready and willing to lift me out of my self-made basement and raise me up.

Thank you, Lord, for your glorious elevator that is always working and is never "out of service."

Shared from the Heart

We all know that there will be times when we feel down. Life can bring things upon us that can literally bring us to our knees. These are the times when we can depend on God the most. All we have to do is call out and he will make his presence known.

Scripture Reading: 2 Samuel 22:33-34

"It is God who arms me with strength and makes my way perfect. He makes my feet like the feet of a deer; he enables me to stand on the heights."

Missed Blessings

Dear Lord,

Something came to me this morning that I believe will help me when I struggle with doing nothing or doing something worthwhile.

When I choose to lie down on the couch and read or watch mindless television over reading my Bible, I drive myself crazy thinking I'm doing wrong by not spending that time in your Word. You and I have our time together every morning and many other times during the day just talking so you know that I'm not ignoring you or your Word.

So why feel guilty? Making myself feel guilty is a bad habit, something I've done most of my life. I believe when I'm doing this to myself, Satan couldn't be happier. He loves to see us struggling with guilt and tearing ourselves down.

The cool thing you helped me discover this morning was that reading a book or watching television instead of reading your Word in the evening does not have to be wrong. What it does mean is that I might be missing out on a blessing that you had in store for me through your Word—not sinning, just missing out on a blessing.

I'll try to watch the guilt trips I put myself on but I'll also spend more time at night in your Word because I really don't want to miss any of your blessings!

Shared from the Heart

I try to always have a quiet time with the Lord and his Word in the morning but there are times in the evening when I battle with myself over reading my Bible. I find myself trying to entertain myself with books, television, or computer games.

I have learned that if I really feel the Holy Spirit nudging me to read in the evening, there is usually something special he wants to show me. What a blessing I receive when I'm obedient.

Scripture Reading: John 1:16

"From the fullness of his grace we have all received one blessing after another."

Ordinary or Special?

Dear Lord,

I love the story in John 6 about the feeding of the five thousand. What a miracle. As I was reading, I felt you asking me to look at this story in a different way this morning.

We have a little boy who shared everything he had, both special (fish) and ordinary (bread). He shared with some people he had probably never met before.

The question is: do I do that? Do I take the "special" things in my life and share with others, people I know and ones I don't know? The special things I'm talking about here would be monetary blessings that you give to me on a regular basis.

If I take these "special" things, like the fish, and share with others, there is no doubt that you will sustain me with all the "bread" in life that I need. When this happens, this ordinary bread becomes "special" because it is a provision from you.

So, this means that all the ordinary in my life becomes extraordinary. That's amazing!

Shared from the Heart

I'm learning as I age that God can fill our lives with ordinary things that he can easily turn into extraordinary ones. He loves to provide for us and he loves it even more when he sees his children providing for and blessing each other.

Scripture Reading: John 6:5-13

"When Jesus looked up and saw a great crowd coming toward him, he said to Philip, 'Where shall we buy bread for these people to eat?' He asked this only to test him, for he already had in mind what he was going to do. Philip answered him, 'Eight months' wages would not buy enough bread for each one to have a bite!' Another of his disciples, Andrew, Simon Peter's brother, spoke up, 'Here is a boy with five small barley loaves and two small fish, but how far will they go among so many?' Jesus said, 'Have the people sit down.' There was plenty of grass in that place, and the men sat down, about five thousand of them. Jesus then took the loaves, gave thanks, and distributed to those who were seated as much as they wanted. He did the same with the fish. When they had all had enough to eat, he said to his disciples, 'Gather the pieces that are left over. Let nothing be wasted.' So they gathered them and filled twelve baskets with the pieces of the five barley loaves left over by those who had eaten."

True Repentance

Dear Lord,

You are such a patient God, loving and kind. The passage below in Hosea is talking about those in Israel who turned against you and were not acknowledging you; they were living a sinful lifestyle.

Persistent sin, or a lifestyle of sin, can make repentance impossible. We can get so caught up in sin that we get numb to its presence in our lives and don't even see the wrong in it anymore.

When we are living in persistent sin, we might seek you in a superficial manner but we won't find you. We will only find you when we sincerely turn to you. My study Bible says, "We must turn to you with a heart of integrity when we repent."

True repenting is a two-step process: (1) we have to ask you for forgiveness and we must mean it to our very core, and (2) we have to actually take action and turn from that sin that has us so entangled.

When we do these things, do you know what happens? (I know you know; I guess I'm asking myself.) WE FIND YOU! This I know from experience.

Shared from the Heart

I have heard it said that a person can harden their hearts so much toward God that they can no longer feel his pulling. That, my friend, is a very serious and sad state to be in.

If we ever find ourselves turning away from God, we've got to make an about-face and return to him as fast as we can. We can't lose our salvation but we sure can mess up our relationship!

Scripture Reading: Hosea 5:4-6

"Their deeds do not permit them to return to their God. A spirit of prostitution is in their heart; they do not acknowledge the LORD. Israel's arrogance testifies against them; the Israelites, even Ephraim, stumble in their sin; Judah also stumbles with them. When they go with their flocks and herds to seek the LORD, they will not find him; he has withdrawn himself from them."

Comfort

Dear Lord,

As I journey down the road of grief, I find comfort in your Word—not your typical scripture to be reading to find comfort. I found myself in Habakkuk. He sees injustice all around him and doesn't understand why you were letting it go unpunished.

Where I found comfort was in his declaration, "*Yet I will rejoice in the LORD, I will be joyful in God my Savior*" (Habakkuk 3:18).

When all around are sadness and tears, I will find my joy in you. That's not to say I'm happy but it says that I'm putting my trust in you, for you are worthy.

Why anyone would try to go through a loss of any kind without relying on and talking to you about it is truly beyond my understanding. Like Paul says in 2 Corinthians 1:3-4, "*Praise be to the God and Father of our Lord Jesus Christ, the Father of compassion, and the God of all comfort, who comforts us in all our troubles, so that we can comfort those in trouble with the comfort we ourselves have received from God.*"

If I don't experience your comfort, how can I comfort others? I can't. The good news is that your Word is true. You are the God of all comfort! I feel your arms around me, I feel your tears mixed with mine, and I feel your blessed peace.

Shared from the Heart

My mother passed away when she was a young sixty years of age. I was really upset with God—so upset that I didn't talk to him or read his Word for weeks. I guess I was trying to punish him.

Even though I was really upset and not exactly acting like one of his children, I still received his wonderful comfort, even without asking.

Why did I receive his comfort? Because I'm his child and he loves me and understands how deep my hurt was. He is a very big God and can handle our being mad at him and he will hold us until the comfort is complete.

Scripture Reading: Habakkuk 3:18-19

"Though the fig tree does not bud and there are no grapes on the vines, though the olive crop fails and the fields produce no food, though there are no sheep in the pen and no cattle in the stalls, yet I will rejoice in the LORD, I will be joyful in God my Savior. The Sovereign LORD is my strength; he makes my feet like the feet of a deer, he enables me to go on the heights."

Unconditional/Conditional?

Dear Lord,

I was looking in your Word this morning for the word "unconditional." I've always been taught (and believe) your love is unconditional. As I searched, I could not find the word and the thought came to my mind, "If it's not in the Bible, is your love conditional?" Have I been misled?

I wondered for a second, when I felt your answer. Your answer was, "No, my love is not conditional—I've loved you since before you were ever formed—but my salvation is."

I had to think about that real quick before my mind started going off somewhere it didn't need to go. Yes, I guess salvation is conditional. No, we don't have to work for it; it's a free gift. "*For it is by grace you have been saved, through faith—and this not from yourselves, it is the gift of God—not by works, so that no one can boast*" (Ephesians 2:8-9). But we do have to accept that free gift. We have to choose to believe that Jesus is the only way, as it says in John. The only condition to our salvation is trusting and believing in your work on the cross through Jesus.

Your unconditional love is what allowed Christ to give his life up for me. The only condition to my salvation is to trust in that unconditional love.

Shared from the Heart

Salvation is very hard for some people to grasp because they can't earn it or buy it. We do absolutely nothing besides accept it as a gift. It's God's unconditional love in full swing.

Scripture Reading: John 14:6

"Jesus answered, I am the way and the truth and the life. No one comes to the Father except through me."

Confidence

Dear Lord,

It's true that you will reveal things to me if I ask and when I am truly seeking your wisdom. I've read this passage in Joshua many times but this is the first time I took notice of the spies instead of Rahab.

The last part of verse 14 says, "…*we will treat you kindly and faithfully when the LORD gives us the land.*" Not "if" but "when." Now, there's confidence.

I want to be that confident when I'm trying to conquer my own giants in my life. No wavering or doubting, just plain faith and trust in you.

Think of the things I could conquer if I only had the confidence that those Israelite spies had. Oh, for that confidence.

Shared from the Heart

Have you ever prayed about something and, in the depths of your heart, there was a tiny bit of doubt? I have and I hate it. God doesn't want us to doubt, just to trust and believe.

That doesn't necessarily mean everything is going to turn out the way we think we want it; it just means we have to trust and believe in the faithfulness of our God.

Scripture Reading: Joshua 2:8-14

"Before the spies lay down for the night, she went up on the roof and said to them, I know that the LORD has given this land to you and that a great fear of you has fallen on us, so that all who live in this country are melting in fear because of you. We have heard how the LORD dried up the water of the Red Sea for you when you came out of Egypt, and what you did to Sihon and Og, the two kings of the Amorites east of the Jordan, whom you completely destroyed. When we heard of it, our hearts melted and everyone's courage failed because of you, for the LORD your God is God in heaven above and on the earth below. Now then, please swear to me by the LORD that you will show kindness to my family, because I have shown kindness to you. Give me a sure sign that you will spare the lives of my father and mother, my brothers and sisters, and all who belong to them, and that you will save us from death. Our lives for your lives the men assured her. If you don't tell what we are doing, we will treat you kindly and faithfully when the LORD gives us the land."

Thought Pattern

Dear Lord,

There's something that I fight constantly and probably will until you call me home. There are times when thoughts enter my mind that have no business being there. My struggle is in immediately taking hold of these thoughts and stopping them in their tracks.

When a questionable thought comes to my mind, I should ask myself two questions: (1) Does this thought please or glorify you? (2) What purpose would I be fulfilling with these thoughts?

Satan loves it when my mind is filled with thoughts that are not glorifying to you. The below scripture and my memorization of it will give me ammunition to fight him. You used scripture to fight him when you were here (Matthew 4:4) and I can, too.

It's kind of like mind over matter. I let you and your Word take over my mind and the rest doesn't matter.

Shared from the Heart

Boy, I could have saved myself a lot of heartache if I had memorized Philippians 4:8 when I was young. I learned the hard way that our thoughts can turn into action and our actions can cause us to sin.

God's Word is an excellent way to fight off Satan and keep our thoughts heading in the right direction.

Scripture Reading: Philippians 4:8

"Whatever is true, whatever is noble, whatever is right, whatever is pure, whatever is lovely, whatever is admirable—if anything is excellent or praiseworthy—think about these things."

Joyless

Dear Lord,

This is quite humorous, Lord, but I think I just figured out why I get so upset when I'm driving to work. When cars won't let me on the freeway or let me change lanes as quickly as I think they should, I get this feeling of unimportance. I feel inferior, like a nobody! Well, I said it was humorous. Sounds like a pretty serious inferiority complex if you ask me.

The only good thing that comes out of these "humorous" feelings is the response I feel from you, like: "You're a child of the King; why would you feel unimportant?" or, "You are adored by the Creator of all things and that makes you a somebody!"

All of a sudden, I find myself relaxing and I'm able to put things back into perspective. I'm thinking I might take things a little too personally sometimes when they really aren't meant to be personal at all, like these traffic scenarios.

Little, dumb things like this can empty me of joy and also make me feel unimportant but you keep filling me up. Satan wants to rob me of my joy by using any means he can but I know you will never let me stay "joyless."

Shared from the Heart

I believe God has a great sense of humor. I'm sure he has to be smiling at me the whole time he's filling me with calmness and joy over silly little life experiences. What Satan wants to tear down, God lifts up and fills to the brim.

Scripture Reading: John 10:10

"Satan is here to…steal and kill and destroy but you have come that we may have life and have it to the full."

Mind or Mindless

Dear Lord,

I've never really been one to worry or be anxious a lot, especially as I've matured and learned to trust in your faithfulness. But as I age and things start to happen, I'm finding myself somewhat fearful.

You and I have discussed this fear I have before, but it still comes back periodically. It's the fear of losing my mind. I believe I can handle all the other aging stuff but this one, Lord, I have to admit scares me. I know that growing older doesn't always mean losing your mind but it could happen and after some of the things I've been doing lately, it's making me wonder.

Things like driving down the same freeway every day and all of a sudden not knowing where I am for a few seconds. How about when I found a shoebox in my closet with a brand-new pair of shoes in it that I didn't remember ever seeing before!

I know I can't ignore serious signs, and I won't, but I also know that you are in control. It's not my desire to lose all my faculties but if I'm going to trust you with something as big as my eternity, I think I can trust you with something as little as my brain or mind.

Even if I end up forgetting who I am, you will not. I am confident of that!

Shared from the Heart

I've got to say aging brings on a lot of changes. Some of these changes I could do without. Memory loss is one of them.

I really don't want to put my family through the heartbreak that Alzheimer's or dementia causes. I will do what I can to keep my mind healthy but I have to trust that the Lord will look out for me when I no longer can look out for myself. And trust him I will!

Scripture Reading: Isaiah 46:4

"Even to your old age and gray hairs I am he, I am he who will sustain you. I have made you and I will carry you; I will sustain you and I will rescue you."

Weeping

Dear Lord,

A while back, I wrote to you about "no tears." My heart was breaking but the tears wouldn't come. It appears that you've opened up the flood gates and now they won't stop. But that's okay because every time I have one of my gut-wrenching weeping spells, my soul feels refreshed. My circumstances haven't changed, my sister is still gone, but when the tears stop, I can hear your still small voice saying, "I keep my promises. I am here."

Isn't this just like you? I'm writing about my heart breaking and my daily devotion for today is all about the mansion that my sister is living in right now and about the one that you are building me for the future. Because of our faith in you, we will see each other again.

Okay, I'm going to miss her while I'm here and the tears will come but there's good news. You came, you died, you rose, and one day all suffering will be gone. What a day of rejoicing that will be!

Shared from the Heart

My heart is filled with joy when I think about heaven. Of course, above all, my joy is based on seeing Jesus face to face, but seeing loved ones that we had on earth is going to be quite wonderful.

Heaven will definitely be a place for rejoicing.

Scripture Reading: John 14:1-3

"Do not let your heart be troubled. Trust in God; trust also in me. In my Father's house are many rooms; if it were not so, I would have told you. I am going there to prepare a place for you. And if I go and prepare a place for you, I will come back and take you to be with me that you also may be where I am."

A Smile

Dear Lord,

My deepest desire is to see your face. When I'm seeking to see your face, I'm usually living in your will and that is always a good place to be.

Do you know what I see, Lord, when I see your face? Through my eyes, I see a beautiful face looking back at me with loving eyes and an award-winning smile. That smile is worth it all. It will be a big smile and it will be just for me, no one else.

My heart melts when I visualize standing before you and just seeing love and acceptance through your smile and eyes. I cannot wait until that day. That brings a smile to my face!

Shared from the Heart

There is a song called "I Can Only Imagine" that brings tears to everyone's eyes the first time they hear it. Can you really imagine what seeing Jesus face to face will be like? I get chills just thinking about it.

What I see in my mind is eyes filled with love and a smile filled with acceptance. Oh, what a day that will be!

Scripture Reading: Revelation 22:3-5

"No longer will there be any curse. The throne of God and of the Lamb will be in the city, and his servants will serve him. They will see his face, and his name will be on their foreheads. There will be no more night. They will not need the light of a lamp or the light of the sun, for the Lord God will give them light. And they will reign forever and ever."

Doubt

Dear Lord,

In Numbers 11:18-23, the Israelites were sick of the manna you had been graciously providing for them and wanted meat. We always want something better, don't we? Anyway, then you tell Moses you will supply meat for all the people (six hundred thousand) and Moses doesn't believe it will happen. Now here's your simple question that blows me away: "Is the Lord*'s* arm too short?" Wow!

Let's forget about the Israelites for a minute and look at how many times in my own life I have prayed and, deep down inside, doubted that it would ever come to pass. I certainly didn't admit it but I'm sure the subtle doubts were there.

There's no telling what you would do in my life, or anyone else's, if we were wholly committed to you and doubt-free.

Too bad I let logic take control sometimes and let my faith take a back seat. Is the Lord's arm too short? I think not!

Shared from the Heart

What does doubt really mean? Here's the definition from Webster's Dictionary: "To waiver in opinion or judgment; to be in uncertainty; to be undecided as to the truth of the negative or affirmative proposition; to be undetermined."

I don't know about you but I don't want any part of that definition to describe my faith or trust in the Lord. No doubts here!

Scripture Reading: Numbers 11:18-23

"Tell the people: 'Consecrate yourselves in preparation for tomorrow, when you will eat meat. The LORD heard you when you wailed, "If only we had meat to eat. We were better off in Egypt." Now the LORD will give you meat, and you will eat it. You will not eat it for just one day, or two days, or five, ten or twenty days, but for a whole month—until it comes out of your nostrils and you loathe it—because you have rejected the LORD, who is among you, and have wailed before him saying, "Why did we ever leave Egypt?" But Moses said, "Here I am among six hundred thousand men on foot and you say, 'I will give them meat to eat for a whole month.' Would they have enough if flocks and herds were slaughtered for them? Would they have enough if all the fish in the sea were caught for them?" The LORD answered Moses, "Is the LORD's arm too short? You will now see whether or not what I say will come true for you."""

Fear

Dear Lord,

One verse and one word stuck out for me this morning when I was reading Psalm 34. The word is "all." Verse 4 says: "*I sought the LORD, and he heard me, and delivered me from all my fears.*" Not just one or two or even three but all my fears. As I cling to you and give you my fears, I believe I'm becoming fearless.

A little further down in Chapter 34:15a, you say: "*The eyes of the LORD are on the righteous and his ears are attentive to their cry.*" You weren't just talking to hear yourself talk when you said your ears were open to hear your children's cries. You were serious.

Through my own experiences in life, I have found that you are always there; you are always listening and you are always prepared to remove all my fears—like the fear of darkness that I grew up with and dealt with most of my adult life. An experience that I will never forget no matter how senile I get is when I cried out to you in complete desperation and you heard my cry and took away that fear.

The only fear I want is a holy fear of you—not to be afraid but a reverent fear for the Creator of everything and the deliverer from all my fears!

Shared from the Heart

"All" is a small word with a big impact. In God's realm, it means that he is big enough, strong enough, and loving enough to handle all of our fears, every single one of them, no matter how big or small they are to us and no matter how long we've been hanging on to them.

Scripture Reading: Psalm 34:1-7

"I will extol the LORD at all times, his praise will always be on my lips. My soul will boast in the LORD; let the afflicted hear and rejoice. Glorify the LORD with me; let us exalt his name together. I sought the LORD, and he answered me; he delivered me from all my fears. Those who look to him are radiant; their faces are never covered with shame. This poor man called, and the LORD heard him; he saved him out of all his troubles. The angel of the LORD encamps around those who fear him and he delivers them."

Burnt Offerings

Dear Lord,

I've got to tell you, Lord, some of your Word gets really detailed and really deep. I love it when you take something that I'm reading (Exodus 29:19-46) and show me something simple and personal.

In this passage, you are telling Moses how to consecrate Aaron and his sons for the priesthood. It talks about burnt offerings and how and when to do them—and in great detail, I might add. Burnt offerings were to be continual.

Do I offer you daily burnt offerings? Do I give you all the "stuff" in my life that doesn't need to be there? Do I allow you to burn it off so I can start fresh every morning—a fresh beginning that only you can give?

I believe, Lord, that your Son gave his life as the final blood sacrifice and because of that sacrifice I can offer you all my sin and you will allow it to burn away and you will turn those ashes into beauty.

My offering to you is a heart committed to loving you and committed to sharing with others why I love you so much!

Shared from the Heart

I want to live every day like I've just been given a new lease on life. God offers this to us every morning. All we have to do is give him all the stuff in our hearts and minds that has no right to be there and give our much-coveted authority over to him.

If we do this, our day has a much better chance of being one that we will be proud of and one we wouldn't mind living again.

Scripture Reading: Hebrews 7:26

"Such a high priest meets our need—one who is holy, blameless, pure, set apart from sinners, exalted above the heavens. Unlike the other high priests, he does not need to offer sacrifices day after day, first for his own sins, and then for the sins of the people. He sacrificed for their sins once for all when he offered himself."

Listening

Dear Lord,

I love to read Psalms. It is so filled with beautiful messages, promises, and feelings that I have felt at one time or another. Verse 3 in Psalm 4 says: "*Know that the LORD has set apart the godly for himself; the LORD will hear when I call to him.*"

It doesn't matter if I'm calling out in anguish, in fear, in brokenness, or even in desperation—you hear me. It doesn't matter if I'm up or if I'm down. It doesn't matter if I'm making good choices or bad ones. Nothing that's happening to me or that I'm feeling goes unnoticed by you. You hear me—no ifs, ands, or buts about it—you hear me!

Everyone wants to know that when they have something to say, they are heard. Being heard by you gives me peace and strength to go on. I'm not going through anything alone; that's one of your promises that I have experienced time and time again.

You might be silent while you hold my hand or hold me in your arms but you are definitely listening and for that I praise your holy name!

Shared from the Heart

When someone has something to say, they want someone to listen to them. One of the things I love about God is that he listens to me no matter what I'm saying.

I have to say there are times I can tell in my spirit that he's not in agreement but he gently guides my thoughts in the right direction. He doesn't let me get by with some of my ranting but he does still listen.

Scripture Reading: Psalm 4:1-3

"Answer me when I call to you, O my righteous God. Give me relief from my distress; be merciful to me and hear my prayer. How long, O men, will you turn my glory into shame? How long will you love delusions and seek false gods? Know that the LORD has set apart the godly for himself; the LORD will hear when I call to him."

Conformed and Transformed

Dear Lord,

I sat here and stared at the phrase "*conformed to the likeness of his Son,*" which is found in Romans 8:29. I kept thinking about hearing that expression all the time but what exactly does it mean?

I know it means to strive to be like Christ but I also know it's impossible for me to be perfect, so why try? Trying to do something when you know it's futile doesn't seem real smart. So, if I can't conform to the likeness of Christ, I guess I could just give up and conform to the ways of this world. That would definitely be easier. But that result is not what I'm looking for. I want to know you better, everything about you. I don't want anything to come between us. To be able to do that, I must have the mind of Christ—be conformed to the likeness of your Son. When making decisions, big or little, I have to ask that question that has become very popular recently: what would Jesus do? I've got to admit, if I ask myself that question, I would more than likely make better decisions—more Christ-like decisions.

I'm going to fail while I'm here on earth but I will still strive to be more like your Son. Oh, but one day I will be completely conformed to the likeness of your Son; I will be sinless. It will be the day I get to see Jesus face to face. I will truly be conformed and transformed!

Shared from the Heart

I get upset when I fail or catch myself in a sin. I hate it when reality hits me that I'm not perfect and won't be until I get to heaven.

Does that mean I just accept it nonchalantly when I sin? No way! I ask for forgiveness, get back on my feet, and once again strive to be more like Jesus.

Scripture Reading: Philippians 3:20-21

"But our citizenship is in heaven. And we eagerly await a Savior from there, the Lord Jesus Christ, who, by the power that enables him to bring everything under his control, will transform our lowly bodies so that they will be like his glorious body."

Hope

Dear Lord,

My sister's birthday is tomorrow. She would have been sixty-seven. You know, Lord, how much I miss her. In your comfort, it's just like you to put something in front of me when I need it most.

The quote you put before me was from "Our Daily Bread", a daily devotional that I just love. It says, "When the sunshine of God's love meets the showers of our sorrow, the rainbow of promise appears."

Oh, how true that is. You love me so much that you have not allowed me to mourn all alone. I'm not talking about my family; I'm talking about you mourning with me, every step of the way. As you mourn with me, you cover me with the sunshine of your love.

You are here and you have also given me hope. Hope is my rainbow—hope of seeing my sister again because of our faith in you. But, more than that, the glorious hope of spending and praising you eternally.

Shared from the Heart

What do we have if there's no hope? Not a lot but with God we always have hope.

I can't imagine going through the things we have to go through here on earth without God. He is our only hope for today, our hope for tomorrow, and certainly our only everlasting hope.

Scripture Reading: Psalm 147:11

"The LORD delights in those who fear him, who put their hope in his unfailing love."

Legacy

Dear Lord,

I just read a Psalm that was full of insight and encouragement. As I was reading it, I felt you were showing me that my days are numbered (just like everyone else's). What is important is what I'm doing with those days.

Am I singing for joy and letting people see that joy? Am I making each day matter?

I don't need to be living for the here and now but with eternity on my mind. I want my life to count for something. When I stand before you, I truly want to hear, "*Well done, my true and faithful servant*" (Matthew 25:21).

I want to leave a legacy that my family and close friends would be proud of and one that will encourage them to have one main desire: to love you with all they have and to strive to know you intimately.

I want my granddaughters and great-grandchildren to look back and be able to see my deep love for you and want that same love. I want them to be able to say that their grandmother was totally sold out to Jesus and be proud of that fact.

I want to leave a legacy of a life lived with love for family and friends but, more importantly, an undying love for her Savior.

Shared from the Heart

I want my daughter, my grandchildren, and their children to be able to look back on my life and see one thing: a life filled with love. A love for them but, more importantly, an overflowing love for God. Not a shallow love but one that runs deep into the depths of my soul and overflows in everything that I do and everyone I touch.

Scripture Reading: Psalm 90:12-16

"Teach us to number our days aright, that we may gain a heart of wisdom. Relent, O LORD! How long will it be? Have compassion on your servants. Satisfy us in the morning with your unfailing love that we may sing for joy and be glad all our days. Make us glad for as many days as you have afflicted us, for as many years as we have seen trouble. May your deeds be shown to your servants, your splendor to their children."

To Truly Be Known!

Dear Lord,

I heard a song recently that said, "You know my name, you know my story. You listen to everything I say." My heart just swells with love for you when I sing that song.

What a magnificent truth this is. I'm not just some unimportant person to you. I'm not just one of a zillion people whom you've seen. I'm me and you know my name! Not only that but you know everything about me. You know about my bad decisions and my good ones. You know my story; you know how all those decisions worked out in my life. You know because you were there through them all.

I love all that but I guess you could say the icing on the cake is that you listen to everything I say. When no one else will pay attention to what I'm saying, you do and you care. Even when I'm babbling and not making any sense, you are listening.

"You know my name, you know my story. You listen to everything I say." Amen and amen!

Shared from the Heart

It just amazes me at times to think about the fact that the God of the universe knows me by name. That's just way cool. More than that, he knows everything there is to know about me and he loves me anyway. What a remarkable Savior we have.

Scripture Reading: John 10:2-4

"The man who enters by the gate is the shepherd of his sheep. The watchman opens the gate for him, and the sheep listen to his voice. He calls his own sheep by name and leads them out. When he has brought out all his own, he goes on ahead of them, and his sheep follow him because they know his voice."

Prince of Peace

Dear Lord,

Okay, yesterday was a day that I would have to categorize as "not a good one." With my work load, doctor appointments, unexpected breathing treatments, not so great health news, flashback of sad times, tests with an IV…not a good day except for one thing: I experienced you!

As I was in the diagnostic center having a test done and they started to put the IV into my tiny veins, I started praying, "Please, Lord, help them find a vein the first time for a change." I was getting a little anxious and then it was over—vein found, FIRST TRY!

I started singing my favorite song that I sing to you all the time, "I love you, Lord, and I lift my voice, to worship you, oh my soul rejoice. Take joy, my King, in what you hear, may it be a sweet, sweet sound in your ear."

Then they started rolling me into that tube (the one that reminds me of a casket). I believe I was still singing when another song came to my mind, "You have been King of my glory, won't you be my Prince of Peace?" The full lyric of the song is, "Hold me, Jesus, I'm shaking like a leaf. You've been my King of glory, won't you be my Prince of Peace?" After that breathing treatment they gave me at the doctor's office, I was literally "shaking like a leaf" but you did what the song asks you to do. You held me close and gave me peace.

That's not to say I wasn't totally wiped out by the time I got home but, deep inside, you truly were and always will be my "Prince of Peace."

Shared from the Heart

When everything around us is swirling out of control, there is no need to wonder where the Prince of Peace is. He's right there in the middle of everything with his big arms wrapped around us, soothing our very souls.

Scripture Reading: Romans 8:6

"The mind of sinful man is death, but the mind controlled by the Spirit is life and peace."

Potter

Dear Lord,

A friend of mine said something recently that made me think. She was talking about molding clay in her classroom and how she didn't wear gloves because she didn't like anything between her fingers and the clay.

Isaiah 64:8 says, "*Yet, O LORD, you are our Father. We are the clay, you are the Potter; we are all the work of your hand.*"

I think sometimes I get in the way of your molding process. I allow things to get between you and me that hinder you from molding me into what you want me to be. You always have the best in mind for me but there are times when, because of choices I make, you have to do some major "re-molding." But, as the "Master Potter," you just keep on molding and re-molding—never giving up until there is nothing between your hands and my heart.

Lord, mold me and make me as you will and I will try to stay out of your way!

Shared from the Heart

I've wondered at times what my life would have been like if I had not gotten in God's way while he was busy molding me. I wonder how different it would have been if I had given him free rein instead of partial rein.

I can't change the past but I'm thrilled to know that God can use my mistakes and misinterpretation of his will, turn me around, and set my feet back on his track.

Scripture Reading: Jeremiah 18:1-6

"This is the word that came to Jeremiah from the LORD: Go down to the potter's house and there I will give you my message. So I went down to the potter's house, and I saw him working at the wheel. But the pot he was shaping from the clay was marred in his hands; so the potter formed it into another pot, shaping it as seemed best to him. Then the word of the LORD came to me: O house of Israel, can I not do with you as this potter does, declares the LORD. Like clay in the hand of the potter, so are you in my hand."

Consuming

Dear Lord,

What do I mean when I say, "You are the bigness in my life"? I know what it should mean. It should mean that everything in life that distracts me from you should be considered little and obsolete and doesn't have a chance to be important.

If you were truly the "bigness" in my life, I would be giving you authority to consume me. I would be living a twenty-four/seven prayer life. I would automatically be discussing everything with you no matter the size. I think the main thing would be not "trying" to listen to you but truly paying attention to every nudge you give me, big or small.

How about me not just listening to you but actually immediately obeying you without giving it another thought? No reasoning it out in my mind but just flat listening and obeying.

I believe, Lord, if I'm doing all that, I would be living the life you have planned for me and you would truly be my "bigness" in life.

Shared from the Heart

I wasn't even sure "bigness" was a word when it popped into my head but it is. It means: "property of having a relatively great size."

I want my love and adoration for God to be the biggest thing in my life. I want it to take over everything about the way I live, think, and act. I want it to be bigger than big.

Scripture Reading: 1 Kings 8:61

"Your hearts must be fully committed to the LORD our God, to live by his decrees and obey his commands, as at this time."

Restful Sleep

Dear Lord,

There's nothing better than, after a hard day at the office, coming home, doing what needs to be done, and then going to bed and falling asleep in your arms.

It doesn't matter what state my life or mind is in, the one thing that makes my life complete is knowing that, as I'm falling asleep, you are holding me. I could be crying, I could be trying to cry (tears dried up), I could be laughing, or I could be upset. It doesn't matter because you are definitely there. You are there and you are holding your daughter, rocking her to sleep.

There is no prescription that will give me a better night's rest than being wrapped up in your arms and falling asleep. No matter how old I get, I will never be too old to be held by my caring, heavenly Father.

Shared from the Heart

There's nothing more precious than rocking and singing a little baby to sleep. Watching their little body finally relax and give in to restful sleep is a wonderful experience.

I believe that is how God must feel about us. He's watching us toss and turn with anxious thoughts going through our minds that will not allow us to relax. Then he takes his place and holds us in his arms and whispers, "Everything's okay. I'm here. Just relax in me."

Scripture Reading: Matthew 11:28-30

"Come to me, all you who are weary and burdened, and I will give you rest. Take my yoke upon you and learn from me, for I am gentle and humble in heart, and you will find rest for your souls. For my yoke is easy and my burden is light."

Life Is but a Breath!

Dear Lord,

Sometimes I take the precious life that you have given me for granted. I just go along with life and then all of a sudden, out of nowhere, someone in my extended family dies and shocks me into a reality check.

The reality is that I will die someday, as everyone else will, unless you return first. I'm not afraid of dying but my fear is of dying and not fulfilling my purpose while I'm here.

I should be moved with great passion to be more of a bold witness for you because the fact is we never know what tomorrow will bring, and there are people you have placed into my sphere of influence who need to be reminded about your story and how it affects them.

Lord, I don't want to stand before you someday and be saddened by all the missed opportunities I had—opportunities in which I could have made a difference in someone's life and possibly in their eternity. Please give me the desire, wisdom, and, yes, passion to share your "good news"!

Shared from the Heart

As I mature, there is one thing I know I don't want to do: live in regret. I don't want to talk myself out of doing something good because it will make me uncomfortable, make me step out of my box, or inconvenience me in some way.

I really don't want to live in "Missed Opportunityville." I want to seize the day and any and all opportunities God puts before me.

Scripture Reading: James 4:13-17

"Now listen, you who say, today or tomorrow we will go to this or that city, spend a year there, carry on business and make money. Why, you do not even know what will happen tomorrow. What is your life? You are a mist that appears for a little while and then vanishes. Instead, you ought to say, if it is the Lord's will, we will live and do this or that. As it is, you boast and brag. All such boasting is evil. Anyone, then, who knows the good he ought to do and doesn't do it, sins."'

Daily Needs

Dear Lord,

Here I am, talking about a song again. I truly love being ministered through music. Anyway, this song says, "God is watching over you, as always" and it just made me think about how you supply what I need, always.

Each day is filled with different circumstances that lead to different needs. Today I need healing and tomorrow I may need strength. You take care of each day's needs as they happen. That is a fact that I have experienced and can trust. You never leave me stranded, handling life on my own. I believe, Lord, that you go before me at times and take care of my needs before I even know I need them.

When you supply all my daily needs, do I remember to share that with others so they, too, can see that you are the one and only true God and that you are the only one who will always come through with just the right provision? I hope so.

Shared from the Heart

Does God give me everything I want? No. Does he give me everything I need? Yes.

He is always taking care of me, even when I don't realize I need taking care of. When this happens, I don't need to keep it under wraps but I need to share with others what he has done so they, too, can see what a great God he is.

Scripture Reading: 1 Kings 8:58-60

"May he turn our hearts to him, to walk in all his ways and to keep the commands, decrees and regulations he gave our fathers. And may these words of mine, which I have prayed before the LORD, be near to the LORD our God day and night, that he may uphold the cause of his servant and the cause of his people Israel according to each day's need, so that all the peoples of the earth may know that the LORD is God and that there is no other."

Less of Me

Dear Lord,

My prayer this morning is that you will make my day more about you and less about me.

I pray that each time I'm tempted to be impatient, unkind, and insincere, or any other of the traits that are not a part of who you are, I will think for a change before acting or reacting. If I do that, I am more apt to make the appropriate choices—ones that make you proud and not sad.

I want to be all about thinking first and acting second. That way, because I've asked you when I began my day to empty me of me and fill me with you, there's less chance to make impulsive or bad choices. I like that a lot!

Shared from the Heart

I really do hate reacting first and then thinking. It never turns out right. I can't tell you how many times I have reacted to someone's unkind remarks before thinking it through.

Thinking <u>first</u> takes a lot of practice and a lot of relying on the Holy Spirit to help you handle your reactions positively.

Scripture Reading: Proverbs 16:9

"In his heart a man plans his course, but the LORD determines his steps."

Healing

Dear Lord,

When my multiple sclerosis rears its ugly head, I get all emotional and sort of have my own little pity party. But all I've been able to hear today is, "Write me a love letter." Since I'm pretty sure the devil doesn't want a letter from me, it has to be your small, sweet voice I'm hearing.

I always do feel better after I've written down my feelings to you, so here I go.

There's no other way to start other than "I love you, Lord." Through all of my years of ups and downs, you have been my Rock, my Fortress, my Shelter, and my Hiding Place. When I'm weak, you are strong. When I feel I can't go on, you pull me up and then you hold me steady. That's when the healing truly begins, when I feel your presence all around me, holding me—healing me from the inside out.

No, I'm not healed from my MS but I'm healed from everything I bring on myself during my problem times with this disease: the self-pity, you know, the "why me" stuff that I hate but still do.

All I really know, Lord, is that I can endure all things because you are here, holding me, rocking me back and forth, calming me, and letting me know what I sometimes tend to forget: that you are my Father and I am your child and you are with me now and will be forevermore.

Shared from the Heart

I think one of the saddest statements I've ever heard is that being a Christian is showing weakness. How do you explain to someone that, when I'm weak, there is only one strength I want to rely on and it's certainly not mine?

When I am weak, he is strong and when he's strong, I can do anything through him.

Scripture Reading: 2 Corinthians 12:9

"But he said to me, 'My grace is sufficient for you, for my power is made perfect in weakness. Therefore I will boast all the more gladly about my weaknesses, so that Christ's power may rest on me.'"

Unwanted Stuff

Dear Lord,

Sometimes I deal with some really ugly stuff: greed, envy, jealousy, self-pity, etc. OH, MY GOSH, that's ugly!

So, how then should I overcome this ugliness and come out on the other side? Oh, yes, how about emptying me, Lord, of all the unwanted stuff and filling me with your characteristics? That is something I talk about doing all the time but evidently forget about at times. I want to be filled with things like love, joy, peace, patience, goodness, faithfulness, kindness, gentleness, and the biggie: self-control (Fruit of the Spirit—Galatians 5:22).

You have blessed me abundantly through my lifetime and this greed, envy, jealousy, and self-pity aren't really kind ways for me to say thank you.

Oh, my, I feel much better just knowing that you are busy right now emptying me of the stuff that is not pleasing to you and filling me with all your wonderful characteristics.

Shared from the Heart

To live a life based on the Fruit of the Spirit—love, joy, peace, patience, goodness, faithfulness, kindness, gentleness, and self-control—would be a life well-lived.

Scripture Reading: 2 Peter 1:5-7

"For this very reason, make every effort to add to your faith goodness; and to goodness, knowledge; and to knowledge, self-control; and to self-control, perseverance; and to perseverance, godliness; and to godliness, brotherly kindness; and to brotherly kindness, love."

Glorious Day

Dear Lord,

There's a song in which the chorus says, "Behold, He comes, riding on the clouds, shining like the sun, at the trumpet call. Lift your voice, in the year of jubilee, out of Zion's hill salvation comes."

I wake up in the mornings a lot of times with that chorus on my mind and this morning I started to think about that statement and it brought a big smile to my face and my heart.

One day you will be coming through the clouds (Revelation 1:7) in all your glory and beauty, gathering all those who have put their trust in you. What a glorious day that will be. That just makes me want to stand up and say, "Hallelujah!"

Along with that fact comes a great responsibility. How many people, in my sphere of influence, are not prepared for that wonderful day? There are many good people living good lives but they don't know you as their personal savior.

God, please help me to be a Spirit-filled, loving witness that you want me to be. Don't allow me to be selfish and just be satisfied with my own salvation. Don't let me be satisfied with praying for them but help me to put my words into action.

I'm asking for a heart that wants to make sure anyone whom you put in my path knows about your love, your sacrifice, and your perfect salvation.

That is my heart's desire.

Shared from the Heart

We cannot be satisfied with just being saved. Living a good, clean life is not enough. Praying for others is not enough. God wants us to be his mouth. He wants us to proclaim to the world who he is and what he has done. We cannot be quiet.

Scripture Reading: Isaiah 52:7

"How beautiful on the mountains are the feet of those who bring good news, who proclaim peace, who bring good tidings, who proclaim salvation, who say to Zion, your God reigns!"

The Better Part

Dear Lord,

I've always loved the story of Mary and Martha. Of course, I always wanted to see myself as Mary, putting you first in everything, always paying attention to what you had to say.

As I write this and read the story again, I see (with the help of my study Bible) that it's about priorities. Sometimes I get so wrapped up in doing that my focus slips a little.

For example, the Bible study we just finished at church was wonderful. I got so much out of it; it was perfect timing for our church. I put so much in the daily workbook and getting ready for class that I neglected just sitting and reading your Word and listening to you.

I, like Martha, got all caught up in the preparation instead of paying attention to "the better part."

There was nothing bad happening, I was just missing out on hearing from you because of my busyness.

Help me, Lord, to keep my focus on you and to always keep what you have to say as my top priority, just like Mary did.

Shared from the Heart

It's so easy to get all caught up in doing something that we allow our priorities to get messed up.

It might be something for the Lord that we are doing, but if we are failing to stop and spend quality time with Him, we are missing out.

Scripture Reading: Luke 10:38-42

"As Jesus and his disciples were on their way, he came to a village where a woman named Martha opened her home to him. She had a sister called Mary, who sat at the Lord's feet listening to what he said. But Martha was distracted by all the preparations that had to be made. She came to him and asked, Lord, don't you care that my sister has left me to do the work by myself? Tell her to help me! Martha, Martha, he answered, you are worried and upset about many things, but only one thing is needed. Mary has chosen what is better, and it will not be taken away from her."

First Claim

Dear Lord,

I've often heard it said, "Look in your checkbook and you will see what your priorities are." It's true.

I believe you desire and want to be honored with our first fruits, not our leftovers.

I read somewhere that we should "honor God by giving him the honor of having first claim on our money, talents, and time." These things belong to you anyway but sometimes we claim more ownership over them than is rightfully ours.

Lord, help me to be a good steward of everything I have. I only have it because you have allowed it. Help me to always give back to you and to **never** ignore the needs of others, near or far.

Shared from the Heart

Why do you think God blesses us monetarily? It's not so we can hoard it and keep it for a rainy day. Yes, we have to make wise financial decisions but if we ignore the needs of other people, we will be missing out on a blessing God has for us. This blessing may not be while we are here on this earth but we have God's promise that we will be blessed.

Scripture Reading: Deuteronomy 16:16-17

"Three times a year all your men must appear before the LORD your God at the place he will choose: at the Feast of Unleavened Bread, the Feast of Weeks and the Feast of Tabernacles. No man should appear before the LORD empty-handed. Each of you must bring a gift in proportion to the way the LORD your God has blessed you."

Surrender

Dear Lord,

"I Surrender All" is a great song and a big statement. When I was growing up, this was one of the songs we sang at the end of the service as an "invitation" song. It was an invitation to come and surrender all and become a new person in Christ. I always thought it was an invitation for the lost.

As I look at it now, I see that it should be a daily invitation to all people. Here are the first and third verses:

> All to Jesus, I surrender, all to him I freely give. I will ever love and trust him, in his presence daily live.
>
> Chorus: I surrender all, I surrender all, all to thee my blessed Savior, I surrender all.
>
> All to Jesus, I surrender, make me, Savior, wholly thine. Fill me with thy love and power, truly know that thou art mine.

When I give you authority over my day each morning, I need to be sure that it includes everything—not just partial authority but a complete surrender.

Surrender is never easy no matter how old you get, but, oh, it's so worth it!

Shared from the Heart

No one likes to say, "I surrender" and yet that is what we all must do. I don't believe there is such a thing as "partial" surrender. You are either all in or you're not.

Let's face it: when we surrender our lives over to the Lord, he can handle all our issues, decisions, and everything else so much better than we can. If that's the case, why in the world would we want to control our own lives instead of "surrendering all"?

Scripture Reading: Psalm 37:5-6

"Commit your way to the LORD; trust in him and he will do this: he will make your righteousness shine like the dawn, the justice of your cause like the noonday sun."

Safeguard

Dear Lord,

Well, you did it again. You showed yourself real in my life one more time.

I could have made a really big mess of a situation but you stopped me and told me to trust you. "Wait and trust me," I believe, is what I heard in my heart. I so wanted to jump out there and take care of the situation but, no, you wouldn't let me. Instead, you led me to this verse. Proverbs 3:5 says, "*Trust in the LORD with all your heart and lean not on your own understanding; in all your ways acknowledge him and he will make your paths straight.*"

Thank you so much, Lord, for holding me back. There's not a shadow of a doubt where my restraint came from. You and you alone kept me from almost destroying a very important relationship.

Shared from the Heart

I have found that life works out so much better if I quit doing all the talking and allow God to have a say. He is always right and he is always ready to advise. All we have to do is listen, trust, and obey.

Scripture Reading: Psalm 48:14

"For this God is our God forever and ever; he will be our guide even to the end."

Bandaged and Bruised

Dear Lord,

There's a song, I can't remember the name of it, but it has a line that says, "Here we are bandaged and bruised; here you are, our beautiful King, to heal us." Lord, that is so beautiful. You inspire some really beautiful music.

How many times in my life have I been "bandaged and bruised"? The answer is "many." How many times has my beautiful King healed me? The answer is "every single time."

Life is not always easy; there's always going to be bruising in a world full of humans. But praise be to you for always being where you need to be, ready to not just put a bandage over our hurts but to heal them completely.

I have never been bruised or deeply hurt that you have not offered healing. Sometimes I licked my wounds for a while first but when I was ready, you healed me.

The power of your healing hand is beyond understanding but is always needed and always accepted, by me anyway.

Shared from the Heart

Sometimes when I am deeply hurt, I like to wallow in my misery before asking for help. Why I do that I can't tell you but I can tell you God loves mending his broken children and does offer healing. We may not receive immediate healing but it will come…and it will come on his timeframe.

Scripture Reading: Jeremiah 33:6

"Nevertheless, I will bring health and healing to it; I will heal my people and will let them enjoy abundant peace and security."

The Reason for the Season

Dear Lord,

There's a popular saying that you see on things and hear all the time this time of year. The saying is: "Jesus is the reason for the season."

This morning, I woke up with a song on my mind and one of the verses says, "We are the reason He suffered and died." The first thing that went through my head was, "we are the reason for the season." That is great!

If it had not been for your perfect plan to reconcile us to you, there would not have been a "season"; there would not have been a miraculous birth one starry night in Bethlehem. We would all just be wandering around with our sins, without hope.

The very "good news" is that you did come to earth as a baby and you did grow up and eventually give the ultimate sacrifice just to reconcile us back to you.

There's our hope: our hope is in that precious baby and in the precious work he did on the cross.

Thank you, Jesus, for coming and for giving and for letting us be "the reason for the season."

Shared from the Heart

Doesn't it just aggravate the daylights out of you to see people wanting to celebrate a Christian holiday of Christ's birth but not wanting to include Christ in it? What good is Christmas without Christ? Doesn't make sense to me!

Scripture Reading: Titus 3:4-7

"But when the kindness and love of God our Savior appeared, he saved us, not because of righteous things we had done, but because of his mercy. He saved us through the washing of rebirth and renewal by the Holy Spirit, whom he poured out on us generously through Jesus Christ our Savior, so that, having been justified by his grace, we might become heirs having the hope of eternal life."

Sunshine

Dear Lord,

"You are my sunshine, my only sunshine, you make me happy when skies are gray." I have not sung that song to anyone in years. Why in the world it came to me today, I have no idea. I just had to laugh when I caught myself singing that to you this morning. Who would have ever thought I would sing that song to you? I might sing it to my granddaughters, but to my Lord? That's kind of humorous.

When I sang it, I meant it. You are what makes my days sunny, even if there are gray clouds in my life. Rather than making me just "happy," I would say you are my joy and my peace, no matter what the day may bring or what clouds may be hanging over me. You are truly "my sunshine."

Shared from the Heart

I'm glad I believe God has a great sense of humor, especially when I'm singing songs to him that would normally be sung to a child. Just like we can receive a message from a song like "Jesus Messiah," he can see our hearts when we're singing to him, no matter what the song may be. It brings joy to him, just like it does to us.

Scripture Reading: 1 Chronicles 16:30-34

"Tremble before him, all the earth! The world is firmly established; it cannot be moved. Let the heavens rejoice, let the earth be glad; let them say among the nations, 'The LORD reigns.' Let the sea resound, and all that is in it; let the fields be jubilant, and everything in them. Then the trees of the forest will sing, they will sing for joy before the LORD, for he comes to judge the earth. Give thanks to the LORD, for he is good; his love endures forever."

Thoughts

Dear Lord,

"Our Daily Bread" gave me a perfect way to always say and do the right thing. It has a title on one of the days that says, "God Be in My Head." I had really never thought about it in that way, but I really like it.

If you are in my head, there won't be those cutting words to bring someone down, all in the pretense of joking. There won't be those defensive thoughts trying to make it out my mouth. There won't be any manipulative ideas to make someone do what I want them to do or any thoughts that are displeasing to you and ones that will eventually hurt me and others.

You need to be in my heart for us to have a relationship but you need to be in my head to keep that relationship where it needs to be—and that is in the very center of my being.

Shared from the Heart

I want my heart and mind to be on the same frequency. My heart belongs to Jesus and I want my mind to reflect that with the thoughts running through it.

I can't really be sold out to him if I'm allowing unkind, selfish, or unholy thoughts to take root in my head.

Scripture Reading: Jeremiah 17:10

"I the LORD search the heart and examine the mind, to reward a man according to his conduct, according to what his deeds deserve."

Mercy

Dear Lord,

I saw this decal on the back of a truck and thought, "What is he thinking?" The sticker said, "Me? I want what's coming to me."

What's that all about? Does he think he's worthy and deserves everything good in life or is he a tough guy who thinks he can handle anything that comes his way?

I have no idea what that stupid sign means. I'm sure it's meant to be humorous but, Lord, it saddened me when I read it. I certainly don't want what would be coming to me if I didn't belong to you and I don't believe this guy does either (I'm assuming it's a guy).

My prayer is that this person knows that you paid the ultimate price to reconcile us back to you so we wouldn't have to receive what would be coming to us.

Thanks, Lord, for your mercy so that we won't "get what's coming to us" and what we deserve.

Shared from the Heart

I love the definitions of "mercy" and "grace." Mercy: not getting what you deserve. Grace: getting what you don't deserve.

Those are two of the most beautiful words in any language. Jesus had mercy and paid the price, which gives us undeserved grace.

Scripture Reading: 1 Peter 2:24

"He himself bore our sins in his body on the tree, so that we might die to sins and live for righteousness; by his wounds you have been healed. For you were like sheep going astray, but now you have returned to the Shepherd and Overseer of your souls."

Trust

Dear Lord,

That was quite something yesterday at work. My manager kept sending me emails reminding me of things, when I had this thought, "When are you going to relax and trust me?" I had to laugh when you turned it back on me and said, "Well, that's what I've been saying to you for a while now."

I don't know why, but sometimes when I can't see the outcome from this side of a situation, I get all anxious and, yes, I worry.

I do trust you, Lord, that I know for sure, but sometimes I put a little emotion in that trust, which makes it look a little like worry.

To use the words from an old hymn, "Oh, for the grace to trust you more."

Shared from the Heart

Getting all anxious and worrying about something does not show our trust in God. He is the one person who cannot and will not betray us. Our trust is safe with him.

Scripture Reading: Isaiah 28:16

"So this is what the Sovereign LORD says: 'See, I lay a stone in Zion, a tested stone, a precious cornerstone for a sure foundation; the one who trust will never be dismayed.'"

Joy

Dear Lord,

What does it really mean to "live in the joy of your salvation"? Psalm 51:12 says, "*Restore to me the joy of your salvation.*" To me it means whenever I let sin in my life, it separates you and me; that separation keeps our relationship from being all it can and should be and I lose that joy (not my salvation, just the joy). The good news is that when I ask for forgiveness, you will restore our relationship.

I can't stop at just being restored. I have to live daily in that restoration. There is nothing that brings joy to my soul more than knowing that there's nothing standing between the two of us. That is deep and abiding joy that I can live in and no one can take from me. It is also a joy that no one or thing can give me but you.

Joy to you, Lord, for you are good and so very faithful!

Shared from the Heart

Sometimes I just live my life without really putting any effort into my relationship with the Lord. I start feeling a little numb inside. That's when I send a quiet prayer up to the Lord asking him to "please restore the joy of your salvation and fill me with your joy." I have never once said that prayer and not received restoration.

Scripture Reading: Psalm 19:8

"The precepts of the LORD are right, giving joy to the heart. The commands of the LORD are radiant, giving light to the eyes."

One Day at a Time

Dear Lord,

"One Day at a Time" was a popular sitcom back in the 1980s that reflected how a single mom dealt with all different circumstances that come up in life. It is also how I am learning to live.

Each day is filled with different situations, different emotions, different feelings, and certainly different actions or reactions.

Psalm 23:1 starts with, "*The LORD is my Shepherd, I shall not want.*" Need I go any further? There is nothing that will come my way that you are not prepared for. If you are prepared then I know I can handle it.

As I empty myself each morning of myself and ask you to fill me with you, I've added this statement, or you could say "plea": "Empty me of me and fill me with everything that you know I will need today."

One day at a time, sweet Jesus.

Shared from the Heart

When everything around me seems to be going crazy, living one day at a time is about all I can do. I have to get up each day and ask for daily guidance and calmness.

There's a song called "One Day at a Time, Sweet Jesus." Here's the chorus:

> One day at a time, sweet Jesus
> That's all I'm asking from you.
> Just give me the strength
> To do every day what I have to do.
> Yesterday's gone, sweet Jesus
> And tomorrow may never be mine.
> Lord, help me today, show me the way
> One day at a time.

Scripture Reading: Philippians 4:19

"And my God will meet all your needs according to his glorious riches in Christ Jesus."

Withdrawals vs. Deposits

Dear Lord,

Life can really be hard. Don't get me wrong, Lord, you've been wonderful to me. You have blessed me my whole life and I know it and praise you for it.

I guess I'm just talking about life in general. There's so much pain, stress, sadness, and disappointment that sometimes I feel like the world is making too many withdrawals from me and I'm just about bankrupt (metaphorically speaking).

Then I realize when I start feeling bankrupt, you start making those automatic deposits—deposits of strength, deposits of peace, deposits of patience, and all other kinds of deposits that you know I need at that particular point in time.

That, my Lord, is way cool!

Shared from the Heart

There are times I feel like my life's bank account is overdrawn or, in gas terms, I'm running on empty. When this happens, I can count on God adding to my account or filling my tank.

He adds all the strength, peace, joy, patience, and any other of his characteristics that he knows I will need to face my current circumstances.

Scripture Reading: Romans 15:35

"May the God of hope fill you with all joy and peace as you trust in him, so that you may overflow with hope by the power of the Holy Spirit."

Just Ask

Dear Lord,

The other day, while talking to you, I was asking you for something that, for the life of me, I cannot remember what it was. It was, however, very important to me at the time.

I know it was important because I wasn't just asking; I was begging. I was getting all worked up when I heard your tender voice in my heart: "You don't have to beg; just ask."

Those words not only brought a smile to my face, as I realized I was begging, but it brought calm to my heart.

I was calm because your words reminded me of who you are. You are the Creator of all things and you can handle all situations that concern me, big or small.

We don't have to beg for intervention; we just have to ask. Ask in faith, knowing you will answer.

Shared from the Heart

I do not ever want to use God like a genie because he is definitely not one. He is, however, a caring Father that wants us to bring all of our needs and concerns to him and trust that he will intervene.

His intervention may turn out to be a little different than what we had asked for but we have to trust in his provision and his wisdom.

Scripture Reading: 1 John 5:14-15

"This is the confidence we have in approaching God: that if we ask anything according to his will, he hears us. And if we know that he hears us, whatever we ask, we know that we have what we asked of him."

Relationships

Dear Lord,

Boy, relationships can really be tough. There are times when they take more energy than I have available.

As I write this, you remind me how important relationships are to you and then you show me through your Word what it takes to make all kinds of relationships be the kind that bring you glory and make you smile.

I've listed a few of your scriptures on some of those needed ingredients that make relationships work:

- Ephesians 4:32—"*Be kind and compassionate to one another, forgiving each other, just as in Christ God forgave you.*"
- Colossians 3:12-14—"*Therefore, as God's chosen people, holy and dearly loved, clothe yourselves with compassion, kindness, humility, gentleness and patience. Bear with each other and forgive whatever grievances you may have against one another. Forgive as the Lord forgave you. And over all these virtues put on love, which binds them all together in perfect unity.*"
- 2 Peter 1:5-7—"*For this very reason, make every effort to add to your faith goodness, and to goodness, knowledge; and to knowledge, self-control; and to self-control, perseverance; and to perseverance, godliness; and to godliness, brotherly kindness; and to brotherly kindness, love.*"
- Matthew 7:12—"*So in everything, do to others what you would have them do to you, for this sums up the Law and the Prophets.*"
- Ephesians 4:29—"*Do not let any unwholesome talk come out of your mouths, but only what is helpful for building others up according to their needs, that it may benefit those who listen.*"

Shared from the Heart

How many truly good and deep relationships have you had in which the other person never showed compassion, forgiveness, humility, or kindness? They never showed godliness, self-control, real love, or encouraged you?

The answer has to be "none" because it takes all these things and more to have the kind of good and lasting relationships that God desires us to have.

Scripture Readings: listed on previous page

What If?

Dear Lord,

There's a lot of stuff going on around me and I'm concerned about the outcome.

All that keeps going through my mind is "what if?" What if I do that? Will that help or hinder things? What if I don't do that? Will that cause hurt to people I love? What if I do it? Will I be appreciated or taken advantage of? Oh, my goodness, I am second-guessing myself all over the place and it's sure not helping anyone!

"What if" is almost as bad as "I can't." I was always told growing up that "can't never could do anything," which made me think twice every time I said it. "What if" is worse because it makes me feel like I'm not trusting you and I'm trying to take care of things on my own.

It's just like you to say something so profound and calming in my spirit just when I need it. You said, oh-so-tenderly, "There are no 'what ifs' in my world." There you have it, plain and simple.

You know what the outcome is going to be and you know what the best decisions are and you won't keep it from me. All I have to do is openly and honestly seek your guidance and you will offer it to me.

It sure takes a lot of pressure off by belonging to you, the one who knows all the paths that I need to take and will guide me down the right one without any second-guessing. When I lay my burdens down and trust you with all things, "what if" does not need to be a concern of mine.

When I finally listen to you, there won't be any "what ifs" in my world either!

Shared from the Heart

I second-guess myself a lot. What if I had done this instead of that or what if I had done that instead of this? If I am truly seeking direction from God, second-guessing would be doubting God's wisdom. I don't know about you, but that's the last thing I want to do. Trust is what it's all about, not "what if."

Scripture Reading: Exodus 15:13

"In your unfailing love you will lead the people you have redeemed. In your strength you will guide them to your holy dwelling."

Focus

Dear Lord,

I was getting all caught up in spending and getting ready for our upcoming cruise when it seems that you felt I needed a little reminder that, although vacations are good and needed for relaxation, I have a tendency to go way overboard and lose my focus and spend all my time, money, and energy on the temporal, or let's say "the here and now."

I really didn't want to hear that because I was really enjoying myself spending all my money so I could look sassy on the ship!

I believe your message to me is that I need to spend a little more time and effort on something that will not burn away once this life is over—something like my character. My character is something I will take on vacation as well as on my eternal trip.

I think Colossians 1:10 sums up what I'm saying very nicely: "*We pray this in order that you may live a life worthy of the Lord and may please him in every way: bearing fruit in every good work, growing in knowledge of God.*"

Shared from the Heart

Sometimes I lack balance or self-control. I get all caught up in "stuff" and let what really counts take a back seat. What really matters is the way I live my life. I should be constantly asking myself, "Is this pleasing to the Lord?" If I'm not consciously trying to live a life pleasing to God and bearing good fruit, I'm missing the boat.

Scripture Reading: Ephesians 5:15-20

"Be very careful, then, how you live—not as unwise but as wise, making the most of every opportunity, because the days are evil. Therefore do not be foolish, but understand what the Lord's will is. Do not get drunk on wine, which leads to debauchery. Instead, be filled with the Spirit. Speak to one another with psalms, hymns and spiritual songs. Sing and make music in your heart to the Lord, always giving thanks to God the Father for everything, in the name of our Lord Jesus Christ."

Faithfulness

Dear Lord,

My favorite attribute of yours that stands out way above all the others would have to be your faithfulness.

I love your provision for me, your protection, your strength, your comfort when my sorrow overwhelms me, your guidance when I so easily start to lean in the wrong direction, and, of course, your love that I feel even when I don't deserve it.

I wouldn't want to live without any of these things but the one thing that ties them altogether for me is your faithfulness. In your Word, you promise me so many things and because of your faithfulness, you never fail to keep any of your promises.

You are faithful in my here and now and you will be faithful at the end of life as I know it, and your faithfulness will reign throughout all eternity.

You are my faithful one.

Shared from the Heart

There are people who make a lot of promises during a lifetime that they fail to keep. Once someone breaks a promise and is unfaithful, it takes a lot to restore the relationship that was shattered by that unfaithfulness.

God makes us many promises and he has never broken one of them. He is faithful to the fullest extent.

Scripture Reading: 1 Corinthians 1:8-9

"He will keep you strong to the end, so that you will be blameless on the day of our Lord Jesus Christ. God, who has called you into fellowship with his Son Jesus Christ our Lord, is faithful."

Falling Apart

Dear Lord,

When I feel my world falling apart with no end in sight, I have to trust and rely on the fact that you are listening to my prayers and cries of anguish.

I also trust and believe that when everything around me feels out of control, you are active—right here in the middle of these circumstances. I believe that you are orchestrating the outcome right now. It doesn't matter if you take care of the problem by resolving it, gently guiding me through it, or just plain holding on to me while it passes. Whichever way it is, I know you are present and listening to my urgent prayers. I also know you care like no one else possibly can.

You are God, you are big, and you are mine. I guess this is not the most spiritual way to put it but I know, because I belong to you, there's a light at the end of the tunnel—and I know without a shadow of a doubt that light is you.

Shared from the Heart

I wouldn't want to face tomorrow if I didn't know for a fact that God is with me through every circumstance, good or bad. What is happening or going to happen is not taking him by surprise nor is it too big for him to handle.

Feel his presence and rely on his faithfulness.

Scripture Reading: Jeremiah 29:12-13

"Then you will call upon me and come and pray to me, and I will listen to you. You will seek me and find me when you seek me with all your heart."

Stagnant

Dear Lord,

Why, I don't know, but lately I've felt stagnant in our relationship—totally my fault. I was going through the motions but the deep desire and peace that used to be there were not there.

Two things happened yesterday and today that, once again, prove your love, care, and presence in my life and further prove that you are always listening to me, even if I don't feel it.

First, knowing something was missing, I prayed yesterday morning for you to help me become the intercessor that you really want me to be for others. Not just an "I'll pray for you" kind of intercessor but the kind that actually goes to your throne and talks to you for these people…and more than just once.

After praying that prayer, the very same day, you put someone in my path who completely shocked me when she asked me to pray for her and her relationship with you. She knew I was a Christian but that's all she knew about me. I was completely blown away by how fast you worked!

The second thing was this morning when you brought me to a very familiar passage that has always been a favorite verse of mine, but today you made it jump out at me. Psalm 51:12: "*Restore to me the joy of your salvation and grant me a willing spirit, to sustain me.*"

Wow! I prayed, you answered, and my joy was restored.

Shared from the Heart

I love journaling. Life is so busy that it's hard to remember all the little things God does for us every day. I really believe that the little things, where God shows his active presence in our lives, are what confirm his love and presence.

I love looking back and seeing all his works of love, protection, and care throughout my entire life.

Scripture Reading: Psalm 92:4

"For you make me glad by your deeds, O LORD; I sing for joy at the works of your hands."

Seeing Clearly

Dear Lord,

I was sitting here having my quiet time this morning and I was surprised at what I saw from where I was sitting. I could not see your face in the picture I have of you on the wall because of a big plant that was sitting on the half-wall separating two spaces. I had to look around or through the leaves to see you clearly.

Oh, my, how many times in my life have I put things between you and me that kept me from seeing or hearing you clearly? I'm afraid there have been many. Sometimes these things had no business being there and those are the things that blocked your view almost entirely. Then there were just "things," not bad things—just plain old stuff that pulled me to the side enough that your view was distorted or maybe just a little fuzzy.

Thank you, Lord, for allowing me to see this analogy. Thank you for taking a simple plant and revealing a truth to me. The truth is that, as a human, I will undoubtedly put things in our relationship that do not belong. The truth also is that you are God and you will always be there to help clear the path and to point me in the right direction.

Lord, only you can give me the strength and power to knock things out of the way that have the potential to separate you and me.

Thank you for my restored vision!

Shared from the Heart

It's so easy for me to get all caught up in busyness, doing things, and then all of a sudden I realize that my attention has been distorted. Yes, I'm still having my quiet times but they seem to be sterile. My head is in it but my heart seems to be somewhere else.

When I realize what is happening, I can turn to one of my favorite verses for refocus. Proverbs 3:5-6 says: "*Trust in the LORD with all your heart and lean not in your own understanding; in all your ways acknowledge him and he will make your paths straight.*"

Scripture Reading: Titus 2:11-14

"For the grace of God that brings salvation has appeared to all men. It teaches us to say 'No' to ungodliness and worldly passions, and to live self-controlled, upright and godly lives in this present age, while we wait for the blessed hope—the glorious appearing of our great God and Savior, Jesus Christ, who gave himself for us to redeem us from all wickedness and to purify for himself a people that are his very own, eager to do what is good."

Impossible

Dear Lord,

Sometimes I forget a simple truth found in your Word. That truth is: there is nothing impossible for you.

I've quoted that many times to others dealing with situations that looked dark and impossible and I said it believing it. So why, Lord, when dealing with my own doubts and fears do I forget about that great advice I give out so freely? I really do believe there isn't anything too big or impossible for you in other people's lives, but when it comes to my own, I allow doubt and fear to take control and stop me cold!

I like to take a simple truth, mix it up with doubt, and end up with fear—fear that allows me to think that if I take on this daunting task, a task that I believe you have asked me to do, I will be a failure and a total embarrassment to myself and maybe even my family.

As I'm writing this, a light bulb just went off and I see what you've been trying to say. You've been saying, "Give your doubt and fear to me and I will turn it into trust, and with your complete trust, we will turn the impossible into a task accomplished."

Forgive me, Lord, for my doubt. Forgive me for not acting like "*I can do all things through Him that gives me strength*" (Philippians 4:13).

You are the "master of impossibilities."

Shared from the Heart

God loves to take what we believe is impossible and turn it into a reality. He can and will prove over and over again that with him all things are possible.

Scripture Reading: Luke 1:34-37

"'How will this be,' Mary asked the angel, 'since I am a virgin?' The angel answered, 'The Holy Spirit will come upon you, and the power of the Most High will overshadow you. So the holy one to be born will be called the Son of God. Even Elizabeth your relative is going to have a child in her old age, and she who was said to be barren is in her sixth month. For nothing is impossible with God.'"

Really Living

Dear Lord,

I don't want to live like a human. I want to live like there is supernatural power within me.

I don't want to live defeated just because sin wraps its arms around me. I want to live in victory because of your power and grace.

I don't want to live in a world full of shame and regret. I want to live like I truly believe and trust in the work of the cross.

I don't want to live in a world of "I'll do it someday." I want to live it out today.

The fact is I do have a supernatural power within me because the Holy Spirit resides inside of me. I can live victoriously because you overcame death and the grave. I can live the life that you desire for me, free of guilt and shame, because of the strength and wisdom you provide on a constant basis.

Yes, I can do all these things because "*the one who is in me is greater than the one who is in the world*" (I John 4:4).

That's good stuff right there!

Shared from the Heart

I don't know about you, but I sometimes allow myself to live like I'm defeated. I allow myself to feel the blame of guilt of past sins. I do it to myself without even realizing what I'm doing.

God wants us to live life victoriously and he gave us the Holy Spirit for us to be able to do just that. I sometimes need a reminder that his power is available and already lives within me. All I have to do is tap into it.

Scripture Reading: Romans 6:4

"We were therefore buried with him through baptism into death in order that, just as Christ was raised from the dead through the glory of the Father, we too may live a new life."

Messing Up

Dear Lord,

I know I don't have to tell you this but sometimes it helps just to write things down. I recently messed up and the worst part is I feel I damaged my witness. If I don't live differently, how can I be effective? How can I make a difference when people have seen my "human side"?

I believe you just revealed something earth-shattering to me. I AM HUMAN! I am going to mess up and I am going to fail but, praise be to you, I don't have to live in those failures.

One of your most beautiful characteristics is your never-ending capacity to forgive. You not only forgive; you pick me up, dust me off, and tell me to keep going and to be sure to forgive myself (a very important step).

Because I know that you are now, and always will be, on my side, I can get up, I can keep going, and I can make a difference!

Shared from the Heart

We are all human and we are going to mess up in our lifetime. The good news is we do not have to live in those failures. God is ready and willing to clean us up and set our feet back on solid ground once again. All we have to do is ask with a sincere heart and it's done!

Scripture Reading: Psalm 145:14

"The LORD upholds all those who fall and lifts up all who are bowed down."

Father's Love

Dear Lord,

Sometimes it's hard to express to you what's going on inside of me. It was a very rough weekend, health-wise, but, as usual, you brought me through.

Who would think, in just a few short moments in time, I could be facing a life-or-death situation?

As I look at it from this side, I see you were showing me once again that there isn't anything that you would not do for me. You gave me peace when I should have felt nothing but terror. You gave me humor when I really didn't feel like being funny. And the whole time, the best thing you gave me was your presence. I felt it the whole time during and after the emergency room visit.

I read a verse to a song this morning that sums everything up. It goes like this: "Think about His love, think about His goodness. Think about His grace that brought us through. For as high as the heavens above so great is the measure of our Father's love."

Amen and amen.

Shared from the Heart

God proves his love to me every single day but some days I see it more than others. When things are spiraling out of control, you can count on your Father's love. It can't be measured and it goes on forever.

Scripture Reading: Deuteronomy 7:9

"Know therefore that the LORD your God is God; he is the faithful God, keeping his covenant of love to a thousand generations of those who love him and keep his commands."

Follow and Feed

Dear Lord,

"Follow me. Feed my sheep." You have told me to do that in your Word. So exactly what does that mean?

I go to church, I read my Bible, I pray, and I try to live a life that is a good example. Follow me? Feed my sheep? Am I doing those two things? Am I listening to what your "still small voice" is telling me? Am I feeding your sheep?

I think I might be falling short on the "feed my sheep" part. What do I have to offer other believers?

Well, to begin with, you have held me and guided me through many experiences in my lifetime that need to be shared. I do believe, Lord, that you want me to share my "love letters" that I have written to you—something that started out as private but I feel you are telling me to share with others.

I pray that these love letters will feed others with encouragement and will bring glory and praise to you, the true "Lover of My Soul"!

Shared from the Heart

I believe it's important to the Lord for his children to encourage and love each other. Life can be hard but we have God and we have our brothers and sisters in Christ. What more is needed?

Scripture Reading: John 21:15-19

"When they had finished eating, Jesus said to Simon Peter, 'Simon, son of John, do you truly love me more than these?' 'Yes, Lord', he said, 'you know that I love you.' Jesus said, 'Feed my lambs.' Again Jesus said, 'Simon son of John, do you truly love me'? He answered, 'Yes, Lord, you know that I love you.' Jesus said, 'Take care of my sheep.' The third time he said to him, 'Simon, son of John, do you love me?' Peter was hurt because Jesus asked him the third time, 'Do you love me?' He said, 'Lord, you know all things; you know that I love you.' Jesus said, 'Feed my sheep. I tell you the truth, when you were younger you dressed yourself and went where you wanted; but when you are old you will stretch out your hands, and someone else will dress you and lead you where you do not want to go.' Jesus said this to indicate the kind of death by which Peter would glorify God. Then he said to him, 'Follow me!'"

CPSIA information can be obtained
at www.ICGtesting.com
Printed in the USA
LVOW11s1148060617
537111LV00001BA/66/P

9 781470 154714